❧ SELECTED POEMS

Sophocles

SELECTED POEMS

Odes and Fragments

Translated and Introduced by
Reginald Gibbons

PRINCETON UNIVERSITY PRESS

PRINCETON AND OXFORD

The translator is grateful for the encouragement and suggestions
received from Stephen Esposito, Brooks Haxton, Gregory Nagy, Stephen Scully,
and William Tortorelli.

The translations of the *Antigone* odes "On Man," "On Fate and the Last of the
Family," and "On Eros and Aphrodite," and of the fragments "The Fullness of the
World," "The Sea," and "On Song" were first published in *Poetry* magazine, and are
reprinted with the permission of the editor. "The Sea" was reprinted in *Harper's*
magazine. The translations of the odes from *Antigone* and the notes to those odes
by Charles Segal are reprinted by permission of Oxford University Press.

Library of Congress Cataloging-in-Publication Data
Sophocles.
[Poems. English. Selections]
Selected poems : odes and fragments / Sophocles ; translated and introduced by
Reginald Gibbons.
p.   cm.
Includes bibliographical references.
ISBN 978-0-691-13024-8 (cloth : alk. paper)
I. Gibbons, Reginald. II. Title.
PA4414.A3G54 2008
882'.01—dc22   2008002082

British Library Cataloging-in-Publication Data is available
This book has been composed in Trump Mediaeval Typeface
Printed on acid-free paper. ∞
press.princeton.edu

Printed in the United States of America

10 9 8 7 6 5 4 3 2 1

To the memory of Charles Segal (1936–2002)

Contents

*For the identifying numbers of the fragments in groups, see Notes under the title of each group.

✿ SELECTED POEMS

Introduction

DESPITE (or because of) his accomplishments and stature as a dramatist, mythographer, and political thinker, we inhabitants of a later world do not usually think of Sophokles first as a poet. Yet if we read all seven tragedies and the fragments of Sophokles, we can begin to sense the overall range of his preoccupations as a poet. In addition to Sophokles' extraordinary and unique way of putting perception, idea and feeling into words, indirectly but very strongly he expresses sympathy for human beings whose great powers, courage, and potential come to brokenness, suffering, and grief. Sophokles, the poet, ponders the harmony or dissonance between human and divine justice. He acknowledges uncertainty, doubt, and fear in the human stance toward the divine. He evidently relishes the sheer variety of language, from spoken immediacy to ceremonial song; and in his odes, a special diction and density of poetic language heighten the power of feeling and our sense that, in a way, fate itself lives within language. Language may sometimes be fate.

Reading Sophokles' odes apart from the plays in which they serve a powerful dramatic purpose could seem reductive; but in reading them separately as poems, we begin to see aspects of Sophokles that are not otherwise so apparent when the odes are read only within the plays—especially in translations that have brought over very little of the poetic texture and movement of the odes. These aspects, these meanings, are more available to us if the odes are translated *as poetry*—by which I mean, in shapes that evoke their original poetic structure, in lines that can be read as lines, and in language chosen not primarily to *explain* what the Greek original says, but for the sake of keeping up with the quick movement of Sophokles' imagery, the unfolding of thought in his syntax, and the progress of feeling in his voicing and narrating. As much as Sophokles can be a dramatic psychologist in his dialogue and plots—revealing motives, loyalties, assumptions, conflicts—he can be a poetic psychologist, too, following the thought and feeling that move by association.

1

As a poet, in some ways Sophokles seems *least* visible to us. Translators and stage directors have worked freely with his plays in order to produce versions that are readable and playable—that is, dramatically satisfying—in terms of the ideas about drama and language of their own times; scholars have produced editions and versions that give the student copious information about, and great insight into, the Greeks and the Greek language. But we do not read poems only for information, or even for insight; we also read poems in order to let our feeling and thinking move, turn, leap by means of poetic figures and forms; we also read for pleasures of language, and to experience the poet's stance toward the world. The poetic translator needs to create some sense of Sophokles the poet.

The richly woven textures of Sophokles' language and the beauty of his poetic structures can never be conveyed fully in translation into modern languages, because his odes, especially, cannot be rendered into any diction and form that adequately represent the complexity and effects of the original Greek. And perhaps no translation of a complete play can produce a very strong impression of Sophokles the poet, if only because many translators seem to be trying to keep the odes from getting in the way of the play. The Greeks could enjoy the rhythm of the interruption of a plot by the odes, which provided moments of reflection and feeling, which created suspense. And they could hear and enjoy the remarkable poetic compression and intricate textures and repeated rhythms of Sophokles' choral odes. But we can no longer hear anything like that even in our own language. The Greeks heard linguistic broadband, so to speak, and while we can listen to several things at once in the midst of our busiest moments, we do not know how to listen to everything that is meaningful, all at once, in a rich poetic text.

The ancient Greeks responded to the tragedies as great, complex poetic performances in several poetic modes, and loved the lines. While Sophokles himself might not have thought of his odes as poems that should be heard or read apart from the plays in which they are sung, I believe that when the poems are read by us this way—we who are informed by a very different sense of poetry than that of Sophokles—then we only gain in our sense of Sophokles' powers and achievement. I do not ask for the odes to be read *instead* of the plays, but only for the odes to be read *as* poems—here *and* also within the plays. To be read as poems means, in translation, to be read as instances of poetic thinking, and for their value as the work of a single temperament, rather than primarily for their dramatic effect. We read Browning's dramatic monologues as "Browning"; we perceive something of the authorial mind of Browning even in the great differences between his various masks in those poems; we read certain remarkable passages in Shakespeare as "Shakespeare," not only as the characters "Hamlet," "Othello," or "Lear."

Even in ancient times, choral odes from the plays might be sung as entertainment, apart from the plays. Presumably at least some of those listening might know, or know of, the tragedy to which the song belonged. But perhaps not always. And the effect could be powerful. Plutarch tells of how, when the Athenians lost their disastrous war against the Spartans, in the battles in Sicily, at least a few of the Athenian soldiers avoided execution or slavery because of their ability to recite Euripides, "for it seems that the Sicilians were more devoted to his poetry than any other Greeks living outside the mother country." This was in 413 BCE, and Euripides, whose works were more popular than those of Sophokles or Aiskhylos, was still alive; Plutarch says some of those who eventually returned to Athens thanked Euripides in person for having saved their lives. If this anecdote were not enough to give us a sense of how powerful a medium poetry was in ancient Greece, there is another, even more relevant to my presentation of translations of tragic odes in this volume. Plutarch also writes that (in 404 BCE) when the Spartan conquerors of Athens were deciding what to do with the city and its inhabitants, and entertaining the possibility of razing the city and enslaving its entire population, "the principal delegates [from the Spartan military allies] met for a banquet, [and] a man from Phocis sang the opening chorus from Euripides' *Electra*, which begins with the lines: 'Daughters of Agamemnon / I have come, Electra, to your rustic court.' At this the whole company was moved to pity and felt that it would be an outrage to destroy so glorious a city, which had produced such great men."[1]

So why not give Sophokles a small book solely for some of his poems in translation? To my knowledge, no translator has ever presented to English-language readers a selection of Sophokles' poems—that is, choral odes from surviving plays—all translated with a consistent aesthetic of attention to the language, rhythm, and structure of the originals. Nor, so far as I know, has anyone ever translated a selection of his fragments in order to draw out of them some of the Sophoklean qualities of poetic thinking, keenness of language, and representation of world, feeling, action, and thought.

II

With other Athenian Greek poets of the fifth century BCE, especially Aiskhylos and Euripides, the other tragic poets whose works survive, Sophokles created and developed tragic drama as in effect a performance poem in several poetic modes, and for multiple voices. The tragedies not only inaugurated western drama, and in so doing brought myth and song into relation with dramatized speech, but also gave heightened use to the choral ode. In fact, tragic drama may have developed out of the performance of choral odes, so tragedy in fifth-century-BCE Athens is poetic in origin as well as in form. Meanwhile, the choral ode, an old and well-established poetic genre, remained very much alive; it continued to be performed on ritual and celebratory occasions at a variety of festivals by many different groups, some far larger than the dramatic choruses.

Fifth-century Athenian tragedies combined dialogue and song; ritual and performance; religious and civic occasions. The tragedies included costume, musical accompaniment, and dance; contests of ideas; characters distinguished from each other psychologically as well as by status, power, and their roles in the plot; a mythology immensely rich in story and in meaning; and different kinds of language, from fast-paced, high-stakes arguments called *stichomythia*, to the special poetic diction of the choral odes. Also, the odes were performed differently from the dialogue: they were sung, not spoken; they were danced while sung; and they were voiced by a group, the chorus, not by an individual actor. I call the tragedies performance poems because they consist of verse, some of it spoken, some of it sung or chanted. The messenger speeches are a kind of miniaturized epic narrative. The set speeches and stichomythia dialogue make poetic and dramatic use of the contests of rhetoric and argument so characteristic of ancient Greek public life. The tragedians wrote not only the choral odes that are sung and danced between episodes in the plays, but also occasional choral passages to be sung as lyric dialogue between the chorus and a tragic character, when heightened emotional intensity saturated a scene. So in addition to the superb stagecraft of Sophokles' tragedies, above all *Oidipous Tyrannos*—the ancient play that has arguably most fascinated the modern world—there is superb poetry throughout his plays as well. Yet most translations of Greek tragedies represent primarily the sense and dramatic force of speech and song, not their poetic qualities. The choral ode, in fact, is the most problematic element for modern translators, directors, actors, and audiences. This translation, however, pursues the virtues of the odes as poems, apart from their dramatic function, and apart from the problems of staging them as musical and danced anthems.

The odes translated in this volume (to all of which I have given titles) are drawn from *Oidipous Tyrannos*, *Antigone*, *Oidipous at Kolônos*, *Aias*, *Philoktetes*, and *Trakhiniai*. (The odes in *Elektra* do not at all lend themselves to being read independently of that play.) The odes were sung and danced in performance by men (fifteen, in Sophokles' tragedies) making up a chorus that might be either male or female, depending on the play. A leader of the chorus might sing some passages solo. What a chorus sings or chants in the odes, or says, chants, or sings in dialogue with characters, does not represent the point of view of Sophokles himself. The role of the chorus is that of another dramatic voice—contesting, yielding, asking, praying—in a dramatic relationship with the main characters. Typically the Sophoklean chorus, while distinct in identity from the audience and with its own allegiances, interests, and particular status (for example, a chorus of old men in *Antigone* and in *Oidipous Tyrannos*, or young unmarried women in *Trakhiniai*), nevertheless offers the audience one point of identification, among others.[2] But the chorus has a poetic role, too—they perform the intensity of language that is characteristic of a highly wrought ode, and this intensity is itself a key element in the spectacle—at times, the most important. (In notes at the end of this volume, I describe briefly the dramatic context of each ode.)

I have translated those complete odes from the surviving plays that have a kind of structural completeness on their own. I have also included two speeches that can be read as dramatic monologues—one by the tragic hero Aias (Ajax, in the Latinized form), which seems almost like an uncanny anticipation of much later poets, from Shakespeare to Robert Browning, and the other by Oidipous at the end of his life, on the effects of the passage of time—expressing sentiments that are not foreign to us.

This volume includes all five odes from *Oidipous Tyrannos*, presented as a poem sequence. Many of us already know the plot of this tragedy, so we can follow the action that is only implicit in the odes. Furthermore, the odes clearly mark the stages of feeling of the whole drama: desperate hope for deliverance from plague; loyalty to Oidipous despite authoritative accusations against him; acknowledgment of the folly of offending the gods; more hope, now foolish and blind; and the realization that if even the heroic Oidipous has brought, however unwittingly, horrific moral pollution into his city, then "nothing that's of mortal men is fortunate." Read in sequence, the five odes enact this emotional arc.

Every ode creates an occasion that is part of the play—sometimes very obliquely—but also different from the play. Charles Segal writes that the "odes are set off from the dialogue by meter, dialect, the musical accompaniment, and dance; they also use a far greater proportion of dense poetical language, gnomic utterances, and mythical paradigms." The gnomic or proverbial utterance—expressing something familiar—fits the Greek poet's impulse to relate the subject or occasion of a choral ode to the timeless realm of general, customary, mythological, or divine truths.

None of the choral odes is lyric poetry in our sense of that genre. Greek lyric poetry was simply poetry accompanied by a lyre—that is, poetry as song (the Greek word for song, *aoidê*, was contracted to *ôidê*, and from this word our word "ode" ultimately derives). Greek poetry included much public performance on public themes: a political satire, an exhortation, a hymn to a god, praise of a famous man, a mythic narrative, a drinking song, an epigram, an erotic song, a song of victory, or a dirge. All choral poems were public, and even personal poems—such as love poems by Sappho—were not as private in ancient Greece as they are in the modern world, since they were not only read privately but also performed publicly for audiences small or large. Because choruses (on all occasions) sing their poems as public performances, the odes in the tragedies sometimes invite us to respond to a claim of—in the words of Charles Segal—"a privileged moral authority, which derives from a heightened awareness of the political or social implications of an action, the ways of the gods, the nature of the world order, or the numinous powers of nature or of passion (such as Eros or Aphrodite) that may redirect or destroy human lives." Although we cannot experience or even completely imagine a poetry so wholly public, with public uses no longer present in our culture, the vividness and energy of language in Sophokles' odes, as well as the movement of feeling and thought, invite us to stand within each poem and move with it, as the dancing chorus do, to recite it and breathe it, to join in its (e)motion.

The ambiguity of Sophokles' tragedies requires an audience that engages with the unresolved and potentially unresolvable conflicts and dilemmas of the main characters; the odes likewise invite an active listener or reader to apprehend unresolved and sometimes contradictory feelings and ideas (as in the odes from *Oidipous Tyrannos*). Segal writes, "The very elusiveness and discontinuity of the choral style express the search for a final meaning that may lie beyond the reach of all the human participants, the chorus included. But the language, imagery and broad scope of the odes express at least the hope that a fuller, more inclusive understanding is possible and accessible to mortals."[3] That is, because the odes are thoroughly poetic in nature, rather than a dramatic imitation of speech, they signify more fully, more ambiguously, and perhaps more lastingly. J.-P. Vernant has observed that the language of Greek tragedies does not attain its greatest meaningfulness in the exchanges *among* characters and choruses on stage; rather, "it is only for the spectator that the language of the text can be transparent at every level in all its polyvalence and with all its ambiguities. Between the author and the spectator the language thus recuperates the full function of communication that it has lost on the stage between the protagonists in the drama."[4] The text is for the audience and the reader, not for the characters themselves. However much the choral odes say to the characters themselves in the drama, they are for the audience. And even if Greek spectators or we modern readers cannot, in fact, grasp all that is in the text "at every level," the odes articulate meanings—familiar or new, clear or uncertain, straightforwardly or with dramatic irony—that reach beyond the characters, and even beyond the plays. Even in translation the odes also offer us as readers the sheer pleasures of image, figures (such as metaphor and metonym), narrative, expressiveness, and structure; they offer us fullness of feeling and thought.

III

We know that Sophokles wrote a treatise, "On the Chorus," but it is lost. We don't know how he worked, but we should not assume that he composed orally. While performers of epic narratives such as the *Iliad* and the *Odyssey* could rely on formulaic phrases, well-established mythological stories, and the use of only one poetic meter, and could in fact recompose episodes as they performed from memory, the authors of tragedies created original, unique works, drawing on myth but also inventing, staging conflicts that might have been only mentioned or briefly described in epic poems, and adding new expressive resources to their language and their art. In an era when Sophokles' friend Herodotos was writing his history, Sophokles too must have written. It is nearly impossible to argue that poems as complex as his odes, with their intricate metrical schemes, variations on key words, and remarkable structures, could have been composed without the advantages of written revisions. And in fact Athens was in the midst of one of the great technological and mental revolutions, from oral culture to writing culture. (In the Athenian tragedies and comedies, there are several interesting allusions to or enactments of reading.[5])

And at some point the tragedies, including of course the odes, would probably have had to be written down so that the lines could be learned by or taught to the chorus and the three actors, even if not all of them were literate. Since the poet also composed the music (for which there was an alphabetical form of notation) and created the choreography for the choruses, the task of composing even one tragedy was very large. Between Sophokles' debut as a tragic poet in 468 and his death in 406, he is likely to have written on average about two plays every year, each requiring music, direction, and choreography! (At the annual dramatic competitions, each of three selected Athenian dramatic poets presented three tragic plays and a fourth, buffoonish play, performed last and relying on the crude sexual and scatological humor of satyrs—male mythological creatures, partly animal.) The Athenian tragic poets lived in a culture of keen verbal memory (which is exactly what Plato thought would be destroyed by the technology of writing) *and* the increasingly widespread practice of writing.

IV

From the lost Sophoklean plays there are also more than a thousand fragments that survive—either as quotations in later authors' works, or as words or lines found on ancient papyrus sheets that were reused as scrap paper or for wrapping Egyptian mummies. The Sophoklean fragments range in size from one word to a substantial portion of a satyr play. I have translated a few individual fragments as short poems in themselves; others, much shorter, I have assembled into titled groups by organizing the fragments thematically. I have not added anything of my own to these groups of fragments; I use only Sophokles' lines—his language, images, and ideas, his exclamations, his descriptive, dramatic, and discursive phrases.

My impulse is not to try to reconstruct from fragments something that is lost, but to allow fragments to form something new. In the fragments I have chosen, however small, the language, images and ideas still sparkle with the freshness of Sophokles' responsiveness to the human, the natural, and the divine. Because we are acquainted with a huge variety of poetic practices over the centuries, we can read for fragmentary significance, and we can move from one fragment to another using our own imaginative freedom to perceive the many possibilities of meaning in Sophokles' attention to the world. In fact, the themes of my groups of fragments are Sophokles' own, which I came to perceive by reading these remnants of his work repeatedly. They may not necessarily recapitulate the main themes of his plays, but they suggest some of the dominant themes of a poetic mind, evoking these with images and brief utterances. I seek the poetic and imaginative energy that still remains in some fragments; it cannot be found in all, and so this is not a comprehensive collection of them.

Naturally, a different translator might see somewhat different themes or ideas among the fragments, might well make a different selection, and would certainly produce a different sequencing of the fragments in each group. But I believe that in my choices I have been true to Sophokles' language, temperament, and preoccupations.

A handful of shards remain from Sophokles' lost play *Thamyras*, which portrayed the mythological figure of a poet-singer whose story traces the familiar tragic narrative from power or prominence to insolence and then to punishment by the gods. These fragments from *Thamyras* are the only group in this volume taken entirely from one play; they give us a startled sense of how utterly shattered by time all the lost works of Sophokles are.

My purpose in translating the fragments is the same as in translating the odes: to encounter and to respond to Sophokles, the poet. Rescuing some of the fragments by grouping them together makes it possible for us to get a glimpse of his individual manner of poetic thinking—and paradoxically reveals it in a way that is difficult to follow when we read plays that are complete. As readers, we would not deliberately break down the larger work in order to isolate from it a few words at a time in which we sense a certain way of being-in-language. But time itself—the long, ineluctable, destroying passage of it—has left us, from almost all of Sophokles' plays, only a few words. The fragments are plays in ruins. And so, taking what time has left us, I try to set the fragments next to each other so that not only poetic detail but also poetic delight can be seen again. In the complete odes, by contrast, we are more likely to see his mastery of movement in a poem from one feeling, one image, one idea, to the next (in other words, his mastery of poetic structure), and his surpassing ability to give intimate intensities of feeling a shared and even public urgency.

Our having any fragments at all, much less whole plays of Sophokles, has depended mostly on those who long ago preserved them, never to know that their own quoting of Sophokles, or their schoolboy copying of a Greek text on the back of a discarded document, would safeguard a fragment of what would later be lost. Among those who quote Sophokles in their own works, the reasons for doing so were their own, not ours, within the framework of their own valuation of Sophokles. Early preservation of Aiskhylos, Sophokles, and Euripides served purposes of the cultural and political prestige of Athens. Some of the Athenian tragedies became canonized as school texts in the ancient world and survived for centuries because of it; some were discussed and preserved by later Christian monks, scholars, and thinkers. Lines were quoted regarding flora and fauna, social and material culture, matters of rhetoric and grammar. In what survives of a fifth-century-CE anthology by Stobaeus, the apparently non-Christian compiler of extracts from many Greek writings, the quotations are exemplary statements on morals, ethics, science, and politics (hence my title for one group of fragments, "What Sophokles Wrote on Women Was Preserved by Men"). In his historical and biographical writings, Plutarch quoted Sophokles. But we cannot know if a character whose sober counsel is quoted by Stobaeus or Plutarch, and comes to us only as a fragment of a lost play, was a voice of ideal moderation or a figure like Shakespeare's Polonius whose sentiments are at once more or less truthful and also comically or tragically inadequate. Nor can we know how a statement's position in a drama inflected its meaning either in the typical tragic contest of wills and opinions among characters, or by tragic irony that the audience could perceive and the characters could not. Through various agents, time itself has made its selection of Sophokles' literary remains, and so my choice of fragments is only one more sifting.

V

Sophokles was born in the 490s BCE and died soon after the performance of his last plays, in 406. His life span coincided with the greatest cultural achievements, political institutions, and military successes and failures of the city-state of Athens. He is said to have been an actor and musician as a young man, and to have played the lyre in his tragedy *Thamyras*. With his first plays Sophokles won first prize, defeating the dominant dramatist of his era, the older Aiskhylos. Sophokles often pleased his public—he won many first and second prizes, and never a third. As with other tragedians of his time, his artistic success had a religious and civic dimension unknown in the modern world. Winning a contest of this kind meant being regarded as having contributed seriously and substantially—as well as pleasurably—to public life, honoring the patron god of the theater, Dionysos (in whose theater, beside and below the Akropolis, the Athenian plays were performed), celebrating the dominance of Athens among Greek cities, and offering a performative symbol of Athenian institutions and civic pride. The extent of the public respect given to Sophokles brought him election to the position of military general, and in this capacity he joined an expedition in 440 to punish a rebellious Athenian ally, the island city-state of Samos; Sophokles also held a civic office as a treasurer. Late in life he devoted himself to the god of medicine, Asklêpios.

Sophokles enlarged the earlier form of drama of Aiskhylos in ways that added depth of character and mobility of thought, that focused tragedy on a crucial moment of retrospective insight (or *anagnôrisis*, "recognition") by the central character, and that broadened the range of language in tragedy. From various sources we know that he composed more than 120 plays. Beginning in the European Renaissance, an enthusiasm for the philosophical, scientific, and literary works of the ancient Greeks brought their work into wide circulation among scholars, scientists, historians, political thinkers, philosophers, poets, and dramatists. Sophokles' *Antigone*, especially, came to seem central to an understanding of the possibilities of human thought and political agency (see George Steiner's masterful study *Antigones*). Much later, Freud's focus on *Oidipous Tyrannos* made that play seem again—as it had been for Aristotle, but for different reasons—perhaps the greatest of the tragedies. For us, Sophokles' seven surviving plays represent the genius, talent, cares, and close attention of the playwright, and also many attitudes, preoccupations, and ideas of his age and of later ages as well, since the surviv-

ing plays and the traces of all the lost plays also suggest motives, be-
liefs, and practices of preservers of his work who lived in very differ-
ent historical moments and situations.

VI

Sophokles appears to have been an outwardly conventional be-
liever, neither zealous nor casual, and in his surviving plays he
sometimes puts the gods at a distance. This means that in the odes
he often shows the chorus petitioning the gods to intervene in
human affairs, even though the members of the chorus may see no
clear signs that the gods are listening. On the other hand, it seems
possible to regard the tragic figures in the two greatest plays,
Antigone and *Oidipous Tyrannos*, as responsible in wholly human
terms for what happens to them, and so the choral odes may com-
ment on folly that is wholly human, and may plead with the gods to
remedy human error.

The evidence in literature shows that when a person in ancient
Greece did almost anything, but especially something decisive, ex-
cessive, or impulsive, the gods might be thought to have instigated
it. This is how Sophokles accounts for the madness of Aias. While
Sophokles may also have entertained the idea that at times the gods
withdraw from the human realm, he makes clear that mortals may
nevertheless offend the gods by immoderate and impious words and
deeds. We might think that the god to whom a human act is partly
or wholly attributed is a metaphor for those dimensions of ourselves
that we cannot know fully, or well, or which, even knowing well,
we cannot entirely control. (Ezra Pound said in his early text "Reli-
gio" that the ancient gods are simply enduring states of mind that
we still recognize.) But our secularizing of Greek concepts of divin-
ity does not lessen the truth of Sophokles' writing; instead it only
transfers that truth from religious belief to metaphor. One obvious
example is sexual desire—represented by four poems in this volume.

The Greeks are both alien to us and not so different from us.
There are attitudes we may still share with them which would ex-
plain the odd fact that we do understand so much of their way of
being. On a larger scale, our dominant religions and American polit-

ical institutions, despite their ethical virtues and humane achievements in art, education, and the rights of woman and man, have remained in part as incorrigibly corrupt as were the Greek; and so perhaps we also share the perplexity of the Greeks at how good counsel so seldom prevails in human affairs, despite the fact that prudent and moderate behavior, informed by general shared truths—such as of religion and philosophy and science—can result in less human suffering and greater human good. Again like the Greeks, we so often distrust other human beings whom we consider to be different from us. And traits we still share with ancient peoples (not only in Greece) are many—the determination to destroy and kill, the inclination to worship, the experience of the betrayal of our bodies by illness or age, the reversals of fortune, the feeling of being possessed by wine or song. Even knowing as we do all sorts of hidden reasons for our behavior that the Greeks had not yet thought out, we seem no more able than they to ameliorate enough of what is worst in ourselves in order to commend and foster what is best. Sophokles, among other poets both ancient and modern, articulates ethical and moral questions brilliantly and movingly; he does this obliquely through his characters and choruses. To the chorus singing the Sophoklean ode, and to the audience listening, the stakes mattered, the dilemmas were urgent, and the answers were sometimes not clear—or even when clear, were disturbing.

VII

I translated the five odes from *Antigone* with the late Charles Segal when we made our version of that play. For that volume and for the earlier translation that he and I made of Euripides' *Bakkhai* I wrote essays about some of the problems of translating ancient Athenian plays into present-day English. In the present volume the problems have been different, but, at least to me, no less interesting.

The immediacy and liveliness of Sophokles' language arose partly from the physical world of a culture with the technologies of builders, farmers, fishermen, merchants, shipwrights, and warriors. The Greeks had the metallurgy of war gear and statues and coins, they cut and sculpted stone, they used wheels and writing, and they practiced other arts and crafts that leave few enduring traces at all—paints, cosmetics, cloth, cooking. (Sophokles himself, by the way, was said to have introduced into tragedy something the Greeks called "scene painting," but we don't know exactly what it was.) Ancient Greek is in itself a remarkable source of ideas articulated through, and arising from, figurative language derived from the physical world. Also, it was clearly a very sonorous language, although we do not know exactly what it sounded like. (But we can see that it delighted in sound. For instance, we have the word "gargle," derived from Old French; the corresponding verb in ancient Greek has much more sound: *anagargaridzô*. We have the words "gibberish" and "jibber-jabber," evidently imitative in sound; Spanish has the word *algarabía*, which means gibberish that is foreign, specifically Arabic [!]; Sophokles has on his tongue remarkably harsh-sounding words to mean the incoherent and the alien, such as a word he uses in *Antigone* [line 1002] for the screeching of disturbed birds of augury, a word that conveys that the sound is alien [*barbaros*] and also enacts its meaninglessness by sounding like babble: *bebarbarômenos*. If anything within my small linguistic ken outdoes the rich English stock of words for the everyday world before industrialization—these words having derived mostly from Anglo-Saxon—it is ancient Greek. I wander happily in the lexicon.)

Charles Segal says of the "intricate" poetry of Sophokles that it "often defies translation precisely because it is continually fashioning metaphoric and metonymic links between the realms of nature, the city and the gods. In the *parodos* [introductory or entrance ode] of *Oedipus Tyrannus*, for example, the shrines to which the desperate citizens of the chorus appeal are called 'the shore of the altar,' suggesting, perhaps, safety from the violence of the plague that seems to buffet the city as if it were a ship caught in a seething storm; but this same ode, a few lines before, describes the dark, frightful land of the dead as the 'shore of the western god,' to which the souls of those who perish in the plague fly like birds before a fiery blaze. The figurative language brings together, in a single imaginary landscape, nature (the sea), the city (civic altars), and the gods (the western god, or Hades)."[6]

Sophokles frequently used characters and stories from Homer, and also alludes to other texts. In the famous first line of the first antistrophe (the second stanza) of the third choral ode in *Oidipous Tyrannos* (line 873), Sophokles writes *hubris phuteuei turannon*—which I translate as "Insolence begets a tyrant," which Lloyd-Jones translates as "Insolence has a child who is a tyrant," which Charles Segal translates as "Violence (*hybris*) begets the tyrant," and which R. D. Dawe argued meant "Tyranny begets Hybris."[7] The next line (in my wording) adds: "Insolence, if vainly stuffed with wealth—neither rightfully nor fittingly [. . .]." The implication is that immoderate privilege and wealth corrupt the ruler. It happens that an earlier and renowned Greek poet and ruler, Solon, wrote (in M. L. West's translation), "Surplus breeds arrogance, when too much wealth attends / such men as have no soundness of intent."[8] Another scholar comments on the use of this thought, with very similar wording, by both Solon and the sixth-century-BCE poet Theognis, and translates Solon's Greek this way: "For *koros* [satiety, surfeit] breeds hybris, when much wealth follows all men whose minds are not fit."[9] Clearly, the phrasing and the import are familiar to Sophokles, and he is not only speaking to his audience but also responding to earlier poetry in a way that creates a kind of second, underlying poetic discourse. Similarly, he takes words from Aiskhylos and turns them in a new direction at the beginning of the "Ode on Man" in *Antigone* (see Charles Segal's note on this ode, p. 105, below). And there are many gnomic or aphoristic statements in Sophokles that he gives to characters and chorus when they are appealing to settled custom and accepted truths. For those of us who are not scholars, our experience of encountering Sophokles' poetry lacks this apprehension of allusiveness. (Translation is about culture, too, and our contemporary literary culture lacks a significant practice of poetic allusion, unlike, say, Russian culture, in which poetry is seen by some poets as consisting, as a whole, of a vast "citational epic" in fragments.) My purpose as translator is to try to respond to both Sophokles' way of shaping the poems and also his characteristic vividness of expression. I have not translated freely, adding or deleting; I assure the reader that what is presented here in English I have brought as closely out of the Greek as I could.

VIII

A translation alone cannot make these poems matter to us; some portion of our whole culture must respond, or some region of values within it. I try at least to show what mattered to Sophokles and his time in the form of the public poem and in the articulations of a prodigious poetic mind.

After all, despite differences and difficulties, Sophokles' poems do speak to us, even now in translation. Why? Because we still experience the way poetry works on us in something like the way it did on the Greeks. We too quicken our attention to language, apprehend the strangely potent ways of thinking we call metaphor and metonymy, get pleasure from the sounds of words and the rhythms of phrases, experience a keen interest in following intuitively what a poem says by the way it moves by association from each image or figure of speech, feeling or idea, descriptive or narrative element, to the next. For that matter, why do poets of our own time and language still use poetic devices and structures invented so long ago in other cultures and other languages? I think it is because even a "mental environment" like ours, saturated though it is with the speech and spectacle of commerce, politics, entertainment, and business, has not yet suffocated our responsiveness to the play of language, the compression of meaning, and the power over us, through us, and for us, of all that is extraordinary about language. In our ongoing processes of knowing ourselves, becoming ourselves, knowing others and the world, and surviving in the world, we are immersed in the possibilities of meaning and pleasure in language. Perhaps poetry is an appetite born in human beings when language first came into use, and renewed in each of us anew when we acquire it individually as children. Language-in-poetry can intensify and compress processes of feeling and thought, whether in a lyric, an ode, or a narrative, bringing us to think and feel in particularly meaningful ways. The intensity and play of meaning can make the realm of inner life as large as the outer world. It can strengthen our inner life for trials of mental and physical survival and for the courage required to preserve our ideals of inner freedom and outward action. Poetry deepens the productive silences within us, and points out the emptiness of the noise around us. Dear readers, here is a master of all that, the poet Sophokles.

A note on measure, line and stanza

Unfortunately for us, neither the English language nor the history of poetry in English can provide us with the linguistic and literary resources to create artistic analogues to what Sophokles does in Greek. Since no one can create in English the metrical and rhythmical effects of the Greek originals, because the sounds and rhythmic possibilities of English are fewer, we cannot produce or hear effects like ancient Greek metrical variety and musical complexity. And while we do have a traditional use of end-rhyme, in fact ancient Greek poetry does not use end-rhyme. (But see the note on "On Sleep," p. 108–9.) I use hemistichs (half-lines) when translating the choral odes (free-verse hemistichs in the odes from *Antigone*, which I translated with the late Charles Segal, and syllabic ones in all others). The hemistichs that were once native to our language were used in Old English, an oral culture; they multiplied occasions for the noticeable repetition of sounds. My hemistichs, though, unavoidably belong to late print culture; they multiply occasions for line-initial and line-final typographical emphasis of words, which allows me to emphasize aspects of syntax, rhythm, and sound. (I do try to repeat word-sounds for the sake of weaving the translation together more tightly). My hemistichs do not represent an existing oral rhythm (as in Old English) but rather they are a musical score for ad hoc rhythms and syntax. Why then do I use them? The Greek language is capable of great compression, so English-language translation usually requires more words than the original text. To keep translations to the same line-length as the Greek originals makes the English-language line too long; it sags. But a halved line of two shorter spans remains energetic and allows for four words to be emphasized to the eye (and the mind's ear) by their visual and syntactic prominence at the ends and beginnings of the hemistichs. The very slight hesitations of the enjambments are everything—for rhythmic and conceptual emphasis. I vary the syllable counts of the hemistichs so that in some lines they are of exactly equal length, and in others they are of a strictly counted unequal length. In some of the translations of odes many lines have the same syllabic length; in others, the line length varies.

Why use syllabic counts rather than metrical or free verse? I do not consider metrical verse in English to be at all monotonous when it is excellent, but on the other hand, since English only has one artistically viable metrical foot for sustained use (the iamb), metrical translation of Sophokles' odes would inevitably create a metrical sameness, even if rhythmic variation were more brilliant than I am likely to achieve. However, syllabic (and in the case of the *Antigone* odes, free) verse can allow more variation of the rhythms of our language, while at the same time sustaining closely structured lines and stanzas. (But in the two monologues included in this volume, and in some fragments, I do use iambic meter; translating Greek poetry requires all the resources English verse can offer—syllabic, metrical, and free.) Also, I use hemistichs for the sake of the two-step line as a gesture that might evoke the dance of the original verse— right foot, left; left foot, right. In all the syllabic translations, I produce my syllabic measure not in order to conform to a rule (the rule, in this case, being my own), but rather to produce poetically justified opportunities for emphasis, surprise, and freedom in the lines.

In translating the choral odes, there is another technical problem that is difficult to solve, and very few modern translators have tried to do so. As everyone who has read Greek tragedies (even in translation) knows, the choral odes are usually made up of pairs of stanzas—strophe and antistrophe; the dance that the chorus performs when singing them is thought to have represented a complementary or even antithetical relationship of antistrophe to strophe by moving in one direction in the strophe, and then reversing the steps and moving in the opposite direction in the antistrophe. (An ode may also end with a final stanza, an *epode*, that is not followed by a symmetrical response.) In Greek, strophe and antistrophe precisely match each other metrically, in that each corresponding line—line six, say, of the strophe and line six of the antistrophe—has exactly the same metrical structure. While metrical verse in English sustains the same foot through the line and can only vary the rhythmic pattern by varying the way the natural speech stresses in English, and the pauses for punctuation and emphasis, play against the expected regularity of the meter, each Greek line is composed in a different way, out of the surpassing variety of combinations of different types of metrical feet. So in Greek the metrical responsion, as it is called, in strophe and antistrophe, is dazzlingly intricate.

I attempt only two things: to give each choral stanza in English the same number of lines as the original stanza in the Sophoklean text on which I rely (almost entirely I use the Loeb Library edition by Hugh Lloyd-Jones), and in all the choral odes except those from *Antigone*, to create a syllabic responsion, so that line six, say, of a given antistrophe in my translation precisely corresponds in syllable count and hemistich proportions to line six of the strophe that it answers. When a Greek ode has more than one strophe-antistrophe pair, each pair has its own unique metrical shape; a second pair does not imitate the first pair. And if there is an epode, it too has its own unique metrical scheme. I follow the same practice.

I stay as close as I can to the Greek, or rather to *some* of what the Greek says, since it is impossible to convey it all, and many passages are puzzling either because of textual problems caused by corruption through their having been repeatedly recopied before the invention of print, or because Sophokles' syntax is difficult. I hope I have understood enough of the meaning that is hoarded and released in these extraordinary works to give adequate honor to their maker.

A note on transliteration

I prefer to use transliterations of Greek proper nouns rather than Latinized names; hence Oidipous rather than Oedipus, and many others. It is hard to decide where exactly to draw the boundary, so as not to make names that might be familiar to the reader in their Latin versions unrecognizable when transliterated directly from the Greek. In general, there is no consistency to how translators and scholars use Greek transliteration, or Latin spellings or English words; the same play is known as *Oedipus Rex, Oedipus Tyrannus, Oedipus the King,* and *Oidipous Tyrannos* (or *Turannos*). So there remains some inconsistency in my practice of representing Greek proper names, but I hope only a little. My goal is to represent Greek itself, not Greek filtered through Latin, which would be a little like representing indigenous American proper nouns in their French, Spanish, or English versions, interposing a linguistic barrier to the very sound of the original language (at least so far as we can imagine it.)

❀ DESIRE

O children—She of Kypros is
        Not only called "the Kyprian"
But is named many
        Times with many names.
She's death—and the realm thereof,
        She's undestroyable life,
She's madness raving loose, She's
        Undiluted hot desire,
She is a wailing with pain,
        With sorrow, with rage, with fear.
All real, excellent energy's
        In Her, and all restedness too.
And all that leads us into
        Violence. She pours in, She
Saturates thought and what's
        Inside the breast of all
That has the breath of life.
        For who is not hungry
For this goddess? She goes
        Into the swimming fish,
Into the four-leggèd
        Creatures on dry land, and
Ranging among the birds
        Of omen is Her wing [. . .]
Among wild beasts, and mortals,
        Among the gods up above.
Wrestling Her, which of the gods
        Does She fail to throw three times?
If I have a right to speak
        The truth—and I have the right—
Over what aches in the breast of Zeus
        Himself She rules, and needing no spear-
Shaft nor iron to do it.
        Plans, however many,
Of mortals and of gods, the
        Kyprian cuts to pieces.

Eros, unconquered in   *strophe*
      Combat! Eros, that
Leaps down upon
      The herds! You
That pass the night-
      Watch on a girl's
Soft cheeks, You
      That cross the
Open sea and
      Roam from hut to
Hut in the far
      High fields—neither
The immortals nor
      Man, who lives only a day, can escape
From You, and he
      Who has You
Inside himself
      Goes mad.

You that pull   *antistrophe*
      The reins of just
Minds toward in-
      Justice, disfiguring
Men's lives; You
      That stir up this
Strife between two
      Men of the same
Blood, while victory
      Goes to the force
Of love in the gaze: the
      Desiring eyes of
The bride shine with
      Wedding joy—this Power on its throne rules
Equally with the great
      Laws, for the goddess
Aphrodite at Her play
      Cannot be conquered.

❀ EROS, IMPOSSIBLE TO THWART [fragment 684]

For Eros not only
            Overcomes men and women
Again and again, but
            Agitates even the breath
Of gods up above, and
            Comes and goes across the seas.
Almighty Zeus is not
            Strong enough to ward Eros
Off—He too backs away
            Yet only wants to give in.

🪷 THE MIGHTY KYPRIAN

(Aphrodite presides as Herakles and Akheloüs fight over Deianeira) [Trakhiniai 497-530]

The mighty Kyprian always   *strophe*
      Carries away great victories.
The stories
      Of the gods
I will not mention, nor will I say
      How She deceived the son of Kronos
Or Hades
      The night-swathed,
Or Poseidon,
      Shaker of earth.
But for this bride, what two
      Opponents, not alike
Yet equally potent,
      Stepped down into the ring
To win marriage with her?
      Who went forward into
The conflict thick
      With blows and dust?

One was a powerful river   *antistrophe*
      In monstrous bull-shape, four-leggèd
And with horns
      Angled up—
Akheloüs of Oiniadai—
      While from Thebes, home of Bakkhos, came the
Other with
      Back-curved bow
And shaking the
      Two spears and club
He held high—the son of
      Zeus. Then in combat both
Swarmed into the center,
      Lusting for the girl's bed.

With them at the center
       Was the Kyprian, sole
Bliss-giving judge
       Of such joining.

Then came thud-   *epode*
       Ding of fists,
Rattling of
       Quiver and
Clatter of club on
       Bull's horns, all at once;
And legs gripping
       Belly and hard
Deadly
       Blows from
A forehead and
       Twofold groaning.
And beside a
       Faraway hill
The delicately
       Beautiful one sat
Awaiting
       Her bridegroom.
(I tell this tale as though
       I myself had been there.)
The young bride, object of
       their battle—her anguished
Gazing face awaits
       What the end may be.
Then suddenly she is
       Parted from her mother
Like a lost
       Lonely calf.

✿ THE HUMAN LOT

At many things—wonders,   *strophe a*
         Terrors—we feel awe,
But at nothing more
         Than at man. This
Being sails the gray-
         White sea running before
Winter storm winds, he
         Scuds beneath high
Waves surging over him
         On each side;
And Gaia, the Earth,
         Forever undestroyed and
Unwearying, highest of
         All the gods, he
Wears away, year
         After year, as his plows
Cross ceaselessly
         Back and forth, turning
Her soil with the
         Offspring of horses.

The clans of the birds,   *antistrophe a*
         With minds light as air,
And tribes of beasts of
         The wilderness, and water-
Dwelling sea creatures—
         All these he
Catches, in the close-
         Woven nets he
Throws around them,
         And he carries them
Off, this man, most
         Cunning of all.
With devices he
         Masters the beast that

Beds in the wild and
        Roams mountains—he harnesses
The horse with shaggy
        Mane, he yokes
The never-wearied
        Mountain bull.

He has taught himself   *strophe b*
        Speech and thoughts
Swift as the wind;
        And a temperament for
The laws of towns;
        And how to escape
Frost-hardened bedding
        Under the open
Sky and the arrows
        Of harsh rain—inventive
In everything, this
        Man. Without invention he
Meets nothing that
        Might come. Only from
Hades will he not
        Procure some means of
Escape. Yet he has
        Cunningly escaped from
Sicknesses that had
        Seemed beyond his devices.

Full of skills and   *antistrophe b*
        Devising, even beyond
Hope, is the intelligent
        Art that leads him
Both to evil and
        To good. Honoring the
Laws of the earth
        And the justice of
The gods, to which
        Men swear, he stands

High in his city.
        But outside any
City is he who dares
        To consort with
What is wrong: let
        Him who would do
Such things not
        Be the companion
At my hearth nor have
        The same thoughts as I!

I.

The tribe of man is one,
    One day brought each of us
Into being from a
    Father and a mother.
No better than any-
    One was anyone born.
But some men's only meat
    Is bad luck and hard times;
For others it is wealth
    And well-being; and the
Rest are enslaved under
    The yoke of what must be.

 ~ ~ ~

Accompanying women's lamentation,
    The sound of a flute, not a lyre, is welcome

 ~ ~ ~

Let a man get for him-
    Self, while he lives, as much
As he can of what most
    Pleases him, for the next
Morning always arrives
    Blind to him.

 ~ ~ ~

    His joy made
Him float like wind-
    Blown thistledown

 ~ ~ ~

If you call the whole roll of mortals you will
Not find even one who prospers in all ways

 ~ ~ ~

For the man who's down
                    One night is ten thousand
For the thriving man
                    Each day arrives too soon

~ ~ ~

In the early morning, before
                    The farm servants had even looked—
As I was carrying to the young
                    Goats fresh tender branches I had plucked—
I saw an army marching where the
                    Cape reaches farthest into the sea.

~ ~ ~

Do not marvel, my lord, that I would hold
Onto profit. Even mortals who have
Abundant wealth cling tight to profit: for mortals
Everything else comes second to the money.
Some make much of the man who is not ill.
But I think there is no one who's not ill
Who is poor—for they're always falling ill.

~ ~ ~

Even if the body is a slave's, yet the mind is free

~ ~ ~

What's most painful is when settling things well is
Possible but one ends up hurting oneself

~ ~ ~

Many are the things I envy in your life—
Most of all that you've never been to any foreign land

~ ~ ~

Not even to be is better than to live in the worst ways

~ ~ ~

37

In gardens of
>>> The gods they plough
Only furrows
>>> Of good fortune

II.

A mortal cannot dodge the blow of a god

~ ~ ~

It's noblest to be by nature just. Best is a life
That's free of sickness. Sweetest of all things is this:
The power each day to seize what one most wants.

~ ~ ~

Deliberation has a different purpose than a foot race

~ ~ ~

>>> To be forced
To drink is as bad as being thirsty

~ ~ ~

Persuasion hastens when on the path to evil

~ ~ ~

He who makes the journey
>>> To one in power is
His slave even if when
>>> He set out he was free.

III.

Profit is sweet even if it's from lies

~ ~ ~

All things time lays bare and leads into the light

~ ~ ~

False words bear no fruit

~ ~ ~

Time obscures all things and leads them into oblivion

IV.

I did him in, him yelping like a dog

~ ~ ~

To pull the fetters tight on the hands of a Molossian

~ ~ ~

Battle loves to hunt young men down

~ ~ ~

The whole breed of foreigners loves money

~ ~ ~

                              From his eyes he
Lets fly spear points

~ ~ ~

Head down they hang like songbirds in a net

~ ~ ~

You do not see the enemy
Hovering nearby

~ ~ ~

It's obvious: a runaway slave, when caught,
His ankles fettered, says anything to please

~ ~ ~

He shrieked like a kite
                    Swooping down on fresh meat

~ ~ ~

I am not able to speak [
[. . .]
[. . .]
The stranger [
Not to be believed [

        O Gaia, Mother of the gods
        Not knowing [
        The master of drugs and spells [
The fire-blackened foreigner [
This one and that [
The man with glittering eyes [

   ~ ~ ~

You flatter submissively
        Then you turn and bite, you dog

V.

The tongues of those who are free are free

VI.

The same place in the
        Mind of man holds what
Gladdens and what grieves
        Him—groaning he weeps
Tears even when what
        Happens gives him joy.

   ~ ~ ~

Since, being childless, wifeless, homeless

   ~ ~ ~

No pain like that of a long life

   ~ ~ ~

But if a man could heal his woes by grieving
And with tears raise the dead from down below

Then gold would be less worth having than grief.

~ ~ ~

A man is only breath and shadow

~ ~ ~

A pity—the flute for the dance has stopped

VII.

But my fate turns forever on the fast-
Whirling wheel of the god and changes its nature—
Just the way that in appearance the moon
Cannot stay the same even for two nights,
But first emerges new from indistinctness,
Making its countenance beautiful and full,
And then when it appears the loveliest
It wastes away again and returns to nothing.

~ ~ ~

To open the bolted house-gates of the soul

~ ~ ~

ON SONG [fragment 568]

By Memory's daughters,
>   The Muses,
> Forgetting,
>   Named Lethe, is hated
And not to be loved.
>   O for mortals, what
Power there is in songs,
>   What greatest happiness
That can make bearable this
>   Short narrow channel of life!

WHAT SOPHOKLES WROTE ON WOMEN
WAS PRESERVED BY MEN [fragments]

I.

What I'm guessing at I wish I could see clearly

~ ~ ~

You swear you will give back a favor for a favor?

~ ~ ~

Show sympathy and uphold silence. A woman
Must keep secret what brings shame to women.

~ ~ ~

To those who have good sense, brief speech
To their parents seems most prudent—
Most of all for any maiden born an Argive,
For whom few words, and silence, are a credit.

II.

O women!—boar-faced Ares, blind,
Unseeing, raises a riot of trouble

III.

In what you intend with a man, know like the sea-polyp
On a rock how to change the color of your thoughts

~ ~ ~

It is not right to fill with honey a jar for vinegar

~ ~ ~

A woman swears that she will shun the bitter pain
Of childbirth. But when she's released from this
Hard lot, once more she gets herself caught in the same
Hunting nets, overpowered by a fleeting desire.

IV.

O woman, you who are so shameful and more,
No other evil is or ever will be worse
Than a woman born to give such woe to mortals.

~ ~ ~

And so no keener curse can a man incur than a wife
Who's a calamity, nor anything more select than a wife who's
    correct;
And what each man brooks he speaks of as his luck.

~ ~ ~

What mortal household, even if heaped with fine goods,
Was ever considered happy without a good wife?

~ ~ ~

The promises of a woman I write on water

V.

Now, on my own, I am no more than nothing. But many times
I've looked at woman's nature in this way,
As we are nothing. In childhood, in our father's house,
We live a life that is of all mankind most joyful—
Since the delights of children feed on ignorance.
But when we attain our reason and exuberant puberty,
We are shoved out and sold,
Sent away from our ancestral gods and our parents too—
Some to strangers, some to barbarians,
Some to cheerless households, some to abusive ones.
And after one good-night has yoked us in wedlock,
We must approve all this and think it best.

~ ~ ~

Illnesses too are brought on by despair

🌸 FRAGMENTS OF THAMYRAS

[. . .] the Muses, meeting Thamyris,
the Thracian, on his way from Oikhalía—
from visiting Eurýtos, the Oikhalían—
ended his singing. Pride had made him say
he could outsing the very Muses, daughters
of Zeus who bears the stormcloud for a shield.
For this affront they blinded him, bereft him
of his god-given song, and stilled his harping.
—Iliad 2. 594–600 (translated by Robert Fitzgerald)

The Thracian watchtower of Zeus of Athos

~ ~ ~

Carved foreign lyres and harps—
Sweet-sounding among the Greeks

~ ~ ~

trígônos

~ ~ ~

To this music we foot it
          Forward to sing your praises,
With quick arms and stepping legs

~ ~ ~

Gone now are the songs re-
          Sounding from the plucked harp;
Lyres [. . .] the single pipes

~ ~ ~

At her breast she held a son of Him who goes under the earth—
Autolykos she held, who would thieve many goods from hollow
  Argos

~ ~ ~

kánnabis

~ ~ ~

Destroying the gold-
Encrusted lyre-arms made of horn,
Destroying the harmony of
The tautly strung harp

~ ~ ~

Overcome by an
Irresistible
Mania for music
I rushed to the place
Where men sing—inspired
By the lyres and the rules
Thamyras
Uses to
Make his songs sur-
Pass all others

ON SLEEP
(SUNG FOR PHILOKTETES) *[Philoktetes 828–32]*

Sleep—you that do not know
        How to suffer; Sleep—knowing
Nothing of pain!—come reign
        Over us, breathing sweetly,
Sweetly, favor us, Lord!
        This sunrise radiance that flies
Everywhere, keep it in
        His eyes
And come, come—this I pray,
        Healer and Savior!

THE ODES OF *OIDIPOUS TYRANNOS*

THE CHORUS PLEAD FOR DIVINE AID AGAINST PLAGUE
[First Choral Ode ~ Parados, 151–215]

O sweet-speaking oracle of Zeus, *strophe a*
        Having come down from gold-abundant Pytho
To resplendent Thebes, what is it
You mean? O Delian Healer, to Whom
        We raise our cries, at Your feet I lie in
Weary awe of spirit,
My being shaken by fear. What obligation—
Something new? or something
        That the seasons of the
Year will bring round again?—
Will You exact from me? (Tell me, immortal
        Oracle, O child of golden Hope!)

First I call to You, daughter of Zeus, *antistrophe a*
        Immortal Athena; and to Your sister,
Who guards this land, Artemis of
Good fame, enthroned at the center of the
        Marketplace; and to Phoibos Apollo,
Whose far-striking aim hits
Its intended mark. Appear to me, O You three
Who turn away doom! If
        In the past—when over
This city, destruction
Towered up—You repelled the ruinous flames to
        A far distance, come back again now!

Oh!—I have troubles far beyond *strophe b*
Numbering. A sickness is on all
Of us assembled here. Thought
        Has no spear with which it might turn
Plague away. The offspring of a
Glorious land do not increase;
        And childbirth, as
The women raise their cries, brings to no good end
        Their painful labor.

Watch them—rising up like strong-winged birds, here one,
                    There another, on all sides—
Speed away faster than
                    Inextinguishable
Fires to the headland shores of the god of the west.

Oh!—with all these deaths, far beyond   *antistrophe b*
Numbering, the city itself dies.
On trodden ground her children
                    Sprawl unpitied. Themselves not yet
Mourned, they bring death to more. And wives
And gray-haired mothers, flocking to
                    Altar-shores as
Suppliants—here, there, from all sides—groan from the
                    Pain of their great grief.
Together, their voices, clear and loud, resound
                    In a hymn to the Healer
And in wailing sadness.
                    Golden daughter of Zeus,
For all this, send the welcome face of safekeeping!

And in His ferocity,   *strophe c*
                    May Ares—Who,
Even without His flashing
                    Round bronze shield,
Burns me now as He comes on
                    Amidst shrieking and crying out—
May He be made to turn
                    His back and fly
From our land, let good winds
Push Him to the great mansion of
                    Poseidon's wife
Or at least as far
                    As the Black Sea,
With rough waves and hostile harbors.
(If night fails
                    To accomplish something,

Day comes to it in time.)
Him, O Father Zeus—You
        That bearing fire
Strike down with lightning—
Wither Him with a thunderbolt!

Apollo Lord of Light, may   *antistrophe c*
        Invincible
Arrows from Your braided gold
        Bowstring fill
The air as You stand to shield
        Us, may bright firebrands blaze—torches
Of Artemis, with which
        She darts across
Lykian mountainsides.
And to Him Who binds His hair with
        A golden band,
I plead!—Him Who shares
        His name with this
Land, Bakkhos of the wine-red face,
Companion
        Of Bakkhai who cry out
To Him—I call and call
Him to come near with bright
        Burning pine-torch
Against the god Who
Has, among the gods, no honor!

❧ BUT WHAT DOES THE SEER TEIRESIAS PROVE AGAINST OIDIPOUS?
[Second Choral Ode ~ First Stasimon, 463–511]

Of what man did   *strophe a*
          The oracle
Rock of Delphi
          Chant that with blood-
Stained hands he'd brought
          About something
So unspeakable
          That men cannot
Even speak it?
          Now is the hour
For him to put his
          Foot in flight
With greater might
          Than horses as
Swift as storm winds.
                    For the son of Zeus, armed with
Flames and lightning,
          Leaps down upon this man; and
After him swoop
          The Furies—dread
Fate-spirits that
          Never fail in Their pursuit.

Only a short   *antistrophe a*
          While ago, as
A flash of light
          From snowcapped Mount
Parnassos, the
          Word of gods told
Everyone to track
          Down this man who's
Still undisclosed—
          For he's stealing

Across wilderness,
        Through caves and
Over rocks, be-
        Reaved bull with slow
Foot, alone and
        Striving to outdistance the
Oracles that
        Were uttered at the navel
Of the earth. But
        They, forever
Alive, beating
        Their wings, hover over him.

With dread, with dread,   *strophe b*
        The wise interpreter
Of omens troubles me
        Now, and neither
Approving nor
        Denying his
Words, I do not
        Know what to say,
On I fly with
        Foreboding, not
Seeing what is
        Before me nor
What's behind. For
        Neither now nor
Earlier have
        I learned what strife
There was between
        The Labdakids
And the son of
        Polybos that
It should be the
        One test of him by which I
Determine if
        I should attack

The great repute
               Of Oidipous
And take the side
               Of Labdakids
Regarding deaths
               Whose meaning's not yet disclosed.

And yes—Zeus and   *antistrophe b*
               Apollo are wise: They
Perceive all that pertains
               To mortal men.
But among men
               No certainty
Assures us that
               A seer knows
More than do I.
               One man's wisdom
May exceed that
               Of another.
But never till
               I see what has
Been said proved right
               Will I stand with
Those who condemn
               Him—we witnessed
How that maiden
               With wings came at
Him, that time, and
               He was regarded as wise
And by this trial
               He earned the love
Of the city.
               Therefore I will
Never become
               Convinced that this
Man should be con-
               Victed of acting wrongly.

ON PURITY, INSOLENCE, AND PUNISHMENT
[Third Choral Ode ~ Second Stasimon, 863–910]

May such destiny   strophe a
          Stand beside me that I
Win good regard
          For reverent
Purity in every word
                    And deed—all those established
By super-
          Nal laws, be-
Gotten in high aether, fathered
                    By Olympos alone—for man's
Mortal nature did
          Not engender them,
Nor will
          Forget-
Fulness
          Make them
Sleep.
          It's
In them that God is potent;
                    Nor does He ever grow old.

Insolence begets   antistrophe a
          A tyrant. Insolence,
If vainly stuffed
          With wealth—neither
Rightfully nor fittingly—
                    Rushes up to the topmost
Eaves and from
          The very
Edge must fling itself down to where
                    Useless feet will be of no use.
That which a wrestler's
          Throw made good for the

City
        I ask
The god
        Never
To
        Let
Loose. I will not ever cease
        To hold the god my guardian.

But if a man goes for-   *strophe b*
        Ward arrogantly in
What he does or
        Says, with no fear
Of Justice, nor
        Revering the
Gods' statues
        And temples, then may an
Evil fate
        Get hold of him for his
Disastrous recklessness, if he
        Does not advance his vantage justly,
And does not hold him-
        Self away from what's
Shameful, or if that
        Which must not be touched
He violates heedlessly.
        When things are such, what man can
Avoid the arrow shafts
        Of his own overwrought
Mind? For if
        Acts like these
Are honorable
        Then why
Should I bother to give the
        Gods glory by dancing?

No more will I go with   *antistrophe b*
        Reverence to the earth's

Untouchable
          Navel nor to
The temple of
          Abai nor to
Olympia,
          If these oracles do
Not so fit
                    The way things stand that all
Mortals will point to them. But O
                    Zeus, reigning over all things, Mighty
Ruler—if You are
                    Rightly called so—may
This not escape You
          And Your forever
Deathless sovereignty! For the
                    Old prophecies concerning
Laios are already
          Waning, respected not
At all, and
          Nowhere does
Apollo appear
          With all
The honors due Him. Godly
                    Worship has gone from us.

[Fourth Choral Ode ~ Third Stasimon, 1086–1109]

If I myself   *strophe*
          Am a seer and
Excel
          In judgment,
Then I swear by Olympos
                    That you, Kithairon, cannot
Not learn that to-
          Morrow's full moon
Will not fail to honor you as native
                    Land, nursemaid and mother to
Oidipous, and we
          Will dance in chorus
To give honor
          And praise to you
For favoring
          Our ruler. O Phoibos
Apollo
          To Whom we cry
Out, may
          These things be
Pleasing
          To You!

Who, son, who, from   *antistrophe*
          Among those nearly
Deathless
          Nymphs, lay with
Mountain-wandering Pan and
                    Gave birth to you? Or was it
Some bedmate of
          Apollo the
Loxian?—for He is fond of all wild
                    Pasture in mountain meadows.

Or was it the Lord
      Of Mount Kyllênê?
Or the god of
      The Bakkhai, that
Dweller on peaks
      Who received you as the
Happy gift
      Of one among
Those quick-
      Eyed nymphs He
Most de-
      Lights in?

OIDIPOUS THE CURSED

[Fifth Choral Ode ~ Fourth Stasimon, 1186–1222]

O generations   *strophe a*
    Of mortal
Men, how close to no-
    Thing your life
Is, as I measure
    It. What man,
What man gets hold of
    Enough of
Good god-favored hap-
    Piness that
Is more than merely
    Seeming, and after seeming
Only falls away?
    The lesson
For me of what you
    Were destined
For—you, even you,
    Unhappy
Oidipous—is that
    Nothing that's
Of mortal men is
    Fortunate.

With surpassing skill   *antistrophe a*
    You let fly
Your arrow at its
    Mark and your
Great triumph was not
    In all ways
Favored by the gods'
    Powers (O
Zeus!) when you over-
    Threw that young

Oracle-chanting
        Maiden with sharp curving claws
And for my country
        You stood up
Against death like a
        Tower. For
That, you are called our
        King, held in
The highest honor,
        And it is
You that rule as lord
        Of great Thebes.

But now—whose story is more   *strophe b*
        Horrifying to hear than yours?
Who lives more closely
        Than you with brutal
Burdens and reversals,
        After such upheaval in his life?
O famed Oidipous!—
Fallen into the
Marriage bed that was
Enough—that deep
        Harbor—for son
And father!
(How could it—how?—, your
        Father's
Legacy, that
        Furrow, abide you
So long in silence,
        You wretched creature?)

Time, seeing all things, has found   *antistrophe b*
        You out as you did not foresee;
It has long since judged
        The marriage not a
Marriage, where begetter
        And begotten were one and the same.

O son of Laios!—
I wish and I wish
I'd never seen you!
Loudly I weep

              And from my mouth
I pour out
This sorrow. To speak

              Straight truth:
It was you that

              Restored breath to me—
And you that put the

              Night in my closed eyes.

❧ THE END OF THE FAMILY OF LABDAKOS

✤ ON THE LONG LIFE OF OIDIPOUS
[Oidipous at Kolônos 1211–48]

Whoever longs for   *strophe*
      A greater portion
Of life, failing
      To hold fast to
Due moderation,
      Is standing guard over
Something wrongheaded—
      That's quite clear to me.
For when someone
      Falls into more
Of life than is really
      Needed, the long
Accumulation
      Of the days puts down
Layers of things hard by
      Pain, while you can't
See where what gives us
      Pleasure might still lie.
But then comes He who
      Helps lead everyone
Alike to the end,
      When with no wedding
Song, no lyre, no dance,
      The doom of Hades
Appears—uttermost death.

Not to be born is   *antistrophe*
      Reckoned best of all.
And once one has
      Appeared—to go
As fast as one can
      Back from here to where one
Came from is second
      Best, by far. For while

One is running
                    Through one's youth with
Nimble thoughtlessness held
                    Close in one's arms,
From what repeated
                    Blows does one escape?
What troubles is one not
                    In the midst of?
Murders, betrayals,
                    Squabbles and struggles
And envy! And then
                    What comes last is old
Age—hated by all,
                    Without power or
Company or friends,
                    When ill upon ill
Arrives to live with us.

In such ways   *epode*
                    This man in
Misery—not I
                    Only—like northern
Headlands is battered
                    From all sides by wind-
Whipped winter storm surf;
                    And just so, he's thumped
By dire ruin break-
                    Ing over him, his
Head pummeled without
                    End by waves of it—
Some from where
                    The sun sets,
Some from where
                    It rises,
Some from where at mid-
                    Day it radiates,
Some from northern mountains cloaked
                    In the darkness of the night.

68

❀ ON FATE AND THE LAST OF THE FAMILY
[Antigone 582–625]

Fortunate are they whose   *strophe a*
                  Lives do not
Taste of woe; but among
                  Those whose house the gods
Shake, no ruin is absent
                  As it creeps over a
Multitude of generations like
                  A storm tide of the salt
Sea driven by northern
                  Gales from Thrace—waves
That speed over the ocean
                  Depths dark as the under-
World and churn
                  Up black sand from the sea-
Bed and with harsh
                  Winds hurl it beating
Against headlands
                  That groan and roar.

From ancient times come   *antistrophe a*
                  These afflictions of the
House of the Labdakids
                  That I see falling one
After another onto yet
                  Earlier afflictions of the dead;
Nor does one generation
                  Release another, but some
God batters them instead; nor
                  Do they have any
Way to be set free.
                  The last rootstock of the
House of Oidipous,
                  In light that was spreading,

Is reaped by blood-
                        Red dust of the gods
Under the earth, for foolishness
                        Of speech and a Fury in the mind.

Zeus, what transgression   *strophe b*
                        Of men could overcome
Your power? Neither
                        Sleep that catches
Everyone in its nets
                        Nor the weariless passing
Of the months named
                        For gods can
Overcome it—You,
                        The Generalissimo immune
To time, hold
                        The gleaming marble heights
Of Mount Olympos.
                        For what is now and
What will be after and
                        What was
Before, only one
                        Law can account,
Which is that into the life
                        Of mortal beings comes
Nothing great that lies
                        Beyond the reach of ruin.

It is wide-wandering   *antistrophe b*
                        Hope that brings
Benefit to many
                        Men, but it deceives
Many others with desires
                        Light as air. When
It overtakes
                        A man, he cannot
See clearly until already
                        He has burnt his

Foot on live coals.
                    Wisely someone has
Kept before us the
                    Famous saying that
A moment will come
                    When what is bad
Seems good to the
                    Man whom some
God is driving toward
                    Ruin. Only a short
Time does he stay
                    Beyond the reach of ruin.

❧ OIDIPOUS ON THE PASSAGE OF TIME

(SPOKEN TO THESEUS) [Oidipous at Kolônos 607–23]

O dearest son of Aigeus—only for gods
Is there no growing old and never any death;
All else is blurred to ruin by almighty time.
The strength of one's land withers; strength of body
Likewise; loyalty dies away, disloyalty grows;
And between men and their friends, between one city
And another, the same spirit never stands fast.
At the very first, for some men, and for others
At a later time, good alliances go bad;
Yet then relations are repaired. And if between
You and Thebes there's fair weather now, time as it goes
Will engender countless nights and countless days
In which the pledges of today, sworn right-handed,
Those men, with petty pretexts, will scatter with the spear.
And then my lifeless sleeping body, hidden cold in a tomb,
Will lap up that warm blood of theirs—if Zeus is still
Zeus and if Phoibos, son of Zeus, speaks truth.

If it is right for me   *strophe*
        To revere with praying
The goddess who
        Cannot be seen and
You, Lord of
        Those of the night,
Aidoneus,
        Aidoneus,
Then I pray that
        Without anguish
And tormented
        Fate, the stranger
Will end his journey at
        Those plains of the dead that
Hide everyone away,
        And at the House of Styx.
Many unavailing
        Sorrows having come to
Him, he will be exalted
        Once again by a just god.

O goddesses of earth!   *antistrophe*
        And you—embodied in-
Domitable
        Beast kenneled growling
In your cave
        By the gates through
Which so many
        Strangers pass, you
Unconquered guard
        Of Hades!—as
Ancient story
        Has it. I pray,
O child of Earth and of

Tartarus, that that beast
Will leave the way clear for
                    The stranger making his
Way onto the plains of
                    The dead in the under-
World. To you I call—sleep that
                    Will last an eternity!

✿ HOMELAND EARTH, SEA, AND SKY

Horses, Stranger!—   *strophe a*
      Fine ones—fill this
Country, shining white Kolônos,
      And finest farmsteads. This is where
The nightingale,
      Sweet-voiced songstress,
Sings, lingering,
      As she most likes,
Down greenwood valleys and keeps
      Herself to the
Wine-red ivy
      Of the goddess
And Her treetops:
      Pristine, holy
Places laden
      With myriads
Of ripened fruit—
      Olives and grapes—
Not sun-beaten
      Nor thrashed by storm-
Winds in winter—
      These haunts where, on
The move, Dionysos the Reveler
      Forever treads, with holy
Women who once nursed
      Him still close by him.

The narcissus   *antistrophe a*
      In beautiful
Clusters flourishes for a for-
      Ever of days under dew from
Heaven, the im-
      Memorial
Crown of the great
      Goddesses; and

The gold-gleaming crocus; nor
                    Is there ever
Any slowing
                    Of the limpid
Never-sleeping
                    Streams the River
Kephisos fills,
                    But for all time,
Day after day,
                    Waters quicken
What grows, they flow
                    Transparently
Over the plains
                    Of broad-breasted
Earth. Nor do choruses of the Muses
                    Greatly dislike this place; nor
Does Aphrodite,
                    Holding golden reins.

And there's something such as I have   *strophe b*
                    Never heard of in
Asian lands or the great Dorian
                    Island of Pelops:
A self-originating
                    Plant that springs up with
No care from human
                    Hands, putting fear into
Spears that would attack,
                    Greatly flourishes
In this land—the blue-
                    Gray-green-leafed olive
Tree, nurturer of
                    Boys; no young man nor
Any that dwells with
                    Old age will harm it
Or fell it, for the
                    Ever-seeing eye

Of Zeus Guardian
        Of Temple Olives
Watches over it, as
        Does gray-eyed Athena.

And there is more great praise I can   *antistrophe b*
        Say of our mother
City, a gift of the mighty
        God, a thing of our
Great pride—its glory of good
        Horses, its glory
Of foals, and glory
        Of its power at sea.
O Son of Kronos,
        It was You that set
This country on its
        Throne of pride, You, Lord
Poseidon, who in
        Our roads invented
The bit and bridle
        That gentle horses.
And the oar You made
        For man flies along
Gloriously, leaps
        Ahead, following
The dance of the fifty
        Sea-nymphs' one hundred feet.

THE FULLNESS OF THE WORLD *[fragments]*

I.

Are you traveling
            There by horse? By boat?

~ ~ ~

In storage pits below
            Ground they keep their barley

~ ~ ~

A scorpion stands
            Watch among the rocks

~ ~ ~

Out in the country live
            The caretakers of a
Snake that guards spring waters

~ ~ ~

The dog thistle spreads
            Across all the fields

~ ~ ~

How heavy on everything
            Are the thick cloaking cobwebs

~ ~ ~

Along the shore, ravines,
            Caves, overhanging cliffs

II.

To weave linen robes and tunics

~ ~ ~

In the smoke from a bright
            Altar flame in their streets

Float sweet foreign scents of
                    Myrrh they burn drop by drop

   ~ ~ ~

Bracelets, royal headdresses, a rich coat of fur

   ~ ~ ~

But whip-bait, too, branded thugs, eaters-
                    Of-what-belongs-to-others

  III.

Gray cranes, turtles,
                    Owls, martens, hares

   ~ ~ ~

As in green pale leaves
                    Of a tall poplar—
Even if in no-
                    Thing else—at the top
The morning air moves,
                    Flutters one feather

   ~ ~ ~

Down the steep hills a grazing
                    Antlered deer would come slowly [. . .]
Lifting its nose [. . .]
                    And the fine points
Of its wide rack, easing
                    Itself down unnoticed

  IV.

                    I see you brushing
The dusty coat of the bay horse
                    With a currycomb

   ~ ~ ~

Bring all of it in!
                    Someone knead dough!
Fill a deep bowl! This
                    Man like an ox
That toils does not toil
                    Until he eats!

        ~ ~ ~

Those who love horses and
                    Those who draw bows of horn
And wrestlers on whose shields
                    The little bells jingle

        V.

There was a sheep's fleece, there was from well-treasured vine
And grape a pouring out to the gods, there was an
Offering of every kind of fruit, of barley-groats,
Of the oil of olives, and of the intricate
Work accomplished in wax by the yellow-brown bee.

        VI.

She went rushing on in a bright-hued coat

        VII.

For that task you'll need many bridles
                    And many rudders all at once

❀ *THE SEA [fragments]*

I.

Seafarers I assign
                To the ranks of those most
Beaten down—neither a
                Godly fate nor mortal
Man ever will assign
                To them what they deserve
Of wealth. Always gambling
                Their far-flung trade at long
Odds, they journey many
                Times ruined for profit
They may preserve or they
                May lose. I marvel at
Them, I praise these who go
                Out again always to
Earn a painful poor living
                With their sore, hard-beaten hands.

~ ~ ~

Sailors hauled up the ship's anchor

~ ~ ~

(Yet to a mother, children
                Are the anchors of her life)

~ ~ ~

Gusting hard, the wind came up
                The Ionian sea-lanes

~ ~ ~

As sea pilots sailing by night in fair winds
Are steering with rudders the promising keel

~ ~ ~

Poseidon!—across

        The Aegean,

Inhabiting points,

        Promontories,

Or ruling in

        Your sea deeps,

Wind-raked

        Tides, head-

Lands of rock

        Booming with

Waves

   II.

The wave pushed past me but then in-

        Exorably it pulled me back

   ~ ~ ~

The way lead weights

        Pull the net down, under

   ~ ~ ~

If I could only

        Turn into the soaring

Eagle, climb air far

        Above wastes of water,

High over the swells

        Of the gray-green sea waves

   III.

        Fisherman Palamedes—

Wasn't it he who kept them

        From famine (with the god's own

Help, let it be said), he who

        Invented such clever ways

To kill time while they rested,

        Weary from the hard blows of

Roaring seas—board games and dice,
                Sweet relief from idleness?

   ~ ~ ~

Oh what happiness could you
                Have that is greater than this:
After reaching land, to lie
                Down under the eaves and hear
The steady small rain
                In your sleeping thoughts.

✿ TO DIONYSOS *[Antigone 1115–52]*

God of many names!— *strophe a*
        Glory of the young wife from the clan
Of Kadmos, child
        Of thundering Zeus,
Guardian of magnificent
        Italy, ruling where
The folds of the
        Hills pleat the lap
Of Eleusinian Demeter,
        Shared by all,
You, O Bakkhos,
        That live in
Thebes, mother-city
        Of the Bakkhai,
By the flowing
        Waters of Ismenos
And on the very
        Ground where the
Savage serpent's teeth
        Were planted;

You, Whom the sputtering *antistrophe a*
        Smoking flames of pine-torches have seen,
Up beyond the
        Double peak of
Rock, where the
        Korykian nymphs
Walk with Bakkhic
        Step and Kastalia
Flows down;
        You that the ivy
Slopes of Nysaian
        Hills send forth
To lead them in
        Procession, and the

Green coast rich with
                    Grapes, while immortal
Followers cry out
                    The Bakkhic chant as
You watch over
                    The Sacred Ways of Thebes—

This place that   *strophe b*
                    You and Your
Mother, she who
                    Was struck by
Lightning, honor
                    As highest of all
Cities: now, when
                    The force of
Disease holds the
                    City fast and all
Its people, come
                    Cleanse us! Stride over
The slopes of Parnassos or
                    Cross the moaning narrows to us,

O You that   *antistrophe b*
                    Lead the dance
Of the stars that breathe
                    Out fire, You that
Watch over the voices
                    Sounding in the night,
Child of Zeus, His
                    Son, show us Your
Presence as a god, O
                    Lord, with Your
Bakkhantic Nymphs who
                    Whirl around You in worship
And celebrate You in frenzied dance
                    All the long night, Iakkhos! Generous giver!

❧ THE FATE OF THE HERO

Famed Salamis, wave-beaten   *strophe a*
By white breakers, you abide
    In the sight of all, and with
Blessings of the gods forever!
But in my misery for
    Countless months I have stood fast,
For ages camped in the
    Meadows of Mount Ida,
Bedding down there to sleep,
Worn out by the passage of time,
And with the evil prospect
Of making my journey one day to
    Hated, annihilating Hades.

And I keep my place beside   *antistrophe a*
Aias, who's so hard to help,
    Since now he is joined to a
Madness put in him by a god.
In the past, you sent him out,
    Rushing mighty into fierce
Battle. But now he is
    A lonely shepherd of
The thoughts inside himself,
And grieves for his friends. His great brave
Deeds fall from his hands, he's friend-
Less alongside the unfriendly, woe-
    Ful, unworthy sons of Atreus.

Surely when his mother, so   *strophe b*
    Familiar with old age, and turned
Gray by long years, hears he
    Is ill with what it is that
Eats away his mind,
She'll cry and cry out with grief—
She will not hold herself back
    From the piteous weeping

Of that ill-fated bird, the
Nightingale, but will sing a
Piercing funeral song,
Her hands falling with
Dull heavy blows on her own
Breast and tearing at her long gray hair.

For him who is afflicted   *antistrophe b*
By madness like this, it would be
Better if he hid in
Hades—he who in lineage
Was the noblest of
The war-toiling Akhaians,
But who no longer knows his
Own nature, and lives apart
From it—O poor father, how
Hard for you to endure is
The ruin of your son,
Which now you suffer
To hear, a fate no other
Son of Aiakos ever lived out!

✿ AIAS'S MEDITATION BEFORE SUICIDE
(WITH HIS SWORD IN HIS HAND, AND HIS WIFE TEKMESSA AT HIS SIDE) [Aias 646–85]

Long immeasurable time brings forth all things
From darkness, then hides again from the light
What it has revealed.

     There's nothing that
One should not come to expect. A dread pledge
And the certainty in one's own gut can both
Be overthrown.

     Even I—once as stubbornly
Hard as hot iron that has been plunged in water—
What my mouth says goes soft because of this woman.

Leaving her a widow among enemies,
And my son an orphan, I do feel pity for her.

But I will go to the green meadows by the sea,
To a place of cleansing waters, to wash from myself
The filth of blood so as to escape the heavy rage
Of the goddess.

     I will go further till I find
Some out-of-the-way place and hide this sword
Of mine, the most hate-filled of all arms, I'll gouge
A hole in the earth where no one will see it, and down
There Hades black as night will keep it.

      Since I first
Held in my hand this gift from Hector—of all
My enemies the worst—I've never gotten
Anything good from Greeks.

     What mortals say

93

Is true—that from enemies, gifts are not gifts
And have no good use.

                          From now on we know
To respect the gods as we should and honor the sons
Of Atreus. They are our masters, so one
Must yield to them. How not?—even things
Of awe and greatest force pay due honor:
Snow-deep winter, after all, retreats
Before the summer rich with crops and fruit.
The dismal circle of night yields to the day,
Blazing up with bright light and white horses.
Astounding blasts of storm winds cease and leave
The groaning sea to calm.

                          And all-powerful Sleep
Releases those whom he has shackled—he does
Not hold his prisoners forever. So
Must we not learn to be reasonable,
Somehow?

            I will.
                     But now I understand
That an enemy should be hated only as if
He might someday be a comrade, and that
I should help a comrade only so much
As we help anyone who may not always
Remain one of our own—
                              since most mortals
Cannot put much faith in friendship's harbor.

But all this will turn out well enough in its way.

And you, my wife, go in, and to the gods
Pray that what my heart most wants will be.

I, for one, feel such   *strophe*
                    Pity for him when
I think how with not
                    One fellow mortal to
Care for him, no
                    Companionable
Eyes on him, he lies
                    Infamously disowned,
Forever alone,
                    He suffers, dis-
Abled by a feral canker, dis-
                    Tressed by every need that stands near him.
How—how does
                    Anyone
So ill-fated go
                    On? O devices
Of gods! O disowned
                    Mortal race to whom
The span of life is
                    Stern beyond measure!

This man—who may not   *antistrophe*
                    Be inferior
To any from the
                    Great households—lies alone
And abandoned,
                    Without his share of
Life, afflicted while
                    Far from all others; and
Among creatures with
                    Woolly pelt or
Dappled, he's to be pitied for his
                    Wild pain of body and his hunger:
Without cure,
                    Without care,

Heavily weighed down.
              And Echo, who can
Be seen far off, her
              Mouth never closed, sends
Back to his sharp cries
              Her only answer.

ON HERAKLES

(AT THE END OF THE SONG, THE CHORUS TURN TO ADDRESS
DEIANEIRA) [Trakhiniai 94–140]

You whom the sparkling night   *strophe a*
        Brings forth into the world
Just when her brilliance is
        Stripped from her, you whom she
Blankets well in your bed just
When your fire is flaring—O
Sun! Sun!—you whose bright blaze so
Dazzles—I ask you to tell
        Me, tell me this, please!: Where, where
Is the son of Alkmenë?
        Is he in the sea channels?
Or does he bestride
        Two continents? Say!—
You that to the eye
        Are the mightiest!

Deianeira, I learn,   *antistrophe a*
        Whose body is always
Filled with longing, she for
        Whom two rivals fought, is
Like a sorrowing songbird,
She cannot without tears put
To sleep the longing in her
Eyes, but instead holds in mind
        Her well-remembered fears for
Her husband's journey—she is
        Constantly made distraught by
The desolation
        Of her husbandless
Bed, hoping against
        Some disastrous fate.

For just as one   *strophe b*
                    May see
Untold waves blown
                    By tireless winds,
South or north, into
                    Great swells,
Another and
                    Another approaching and going
Past, across the
                    Broad ocean,
Just so it's the
                    Rough sea of
His life's toils—bringing
                    Honor
To him—that keeps
                    Tossing the
Theban backwards;
                    Yet one of the gods keeps him from mis-
Takes and the house
                    Of Hades.

You dispraise these   *antistrophe b*
                    Things, but
Though I feel in
                    Sympathy with
You, I will contest
                    What you
Say, with respect;
                    For you should not rub and rub at good
Hope till it is
                    Gone. The King
Bringing all things
                    To pass—the
Son of Kronos—did
                    Not set
Down for mortals
                    A freedom

From suffering;
        And the Great Bear's circling path brings round
Joy and pain to
        Everyone.

For mortals, neither   *epode*
        Sparkling
Night nor great trouble
        Nor wealth
Endures—these vanish
        Quickly,
And to this one or
        That come
Rejoicing and loss.
        And so
With regard to these
        Things, I
Say to you, who are Queen, to hold
        Fast, in hope, for who has seen Zeus
Take no thought for his
        Children?

Notes

NOTES TO THE INTRODUCTION

1. Plutarch, *Nicias*, 29 and *Lysander*, 15.
2. Budelmann, especially his last chapter, "The Chorus: Shared Survival," 195–272.
3. Segal 1995, 181,183.
4. Quoted by Budelmann, 4.
5. Svenbro, 366–384, especially 383.
6. Segal 1995, 3–4.
7. Segal 2001, 92; Dawe, 182–83 (this is line 872 in his edition; see his note on that line).
8. West, 76.
9. Irwin, 56.

Works cited in Introduction:

Felix Budelmann, *The Language of Sophocles: Communality, Communication and Involvement* (Cambridge [England]: Cambridge University Press, 2000).

Elizabeth Irwin, "The Transgressive Elegy of Solon?," in *Solon of Athens: New Historical and Philological Approaches*, edited by Joseph H. Blok and André P. M. H. Lardinois (Leiden: Brill, 2006), pp. 36–78.

Plutarch, *The Rise and Fall of Athens: Nine Greek Lives*, translated with an introduction by Ian Scott-Kilvert (New York: Penguin, 1960).

Charles Segal, *Sophocles' Tragic World: Divinity, Nature, Society* (Cambridge [Mass.]: Harvard University Press, 1995).

Charles Segal, *Oedipus Tyrannus: Tragic Heroism and the Limits of Knowledge* (New York: Oxford University Press, 2001).

Sophocles, *Oedipus Rex*, edited by R. D. Dawe (Cambridge [England]: Cambridge University Press, 1982).

Jasper Svenbro, "The 'Interior Voice': On the Invention of Silent Reading," in *Nothing to Do with Dionysus? Athenian Drama in its Social Context*, edited by John J. Winkler and Froma I. Zeitlin (Princeton: Princeton University Press, 1990), pp. 366–84.

M. L. West, *Greek Lyric Poetry* (Oxford: Oxford University Press, 1994).

Suggested reading in addition to Segal, above:

John Herington, *Poetry Into Drama: Early Tragedy and the Greek Poetic Tradition* (Berkeley: University of California Press, 1985).

Sophocles, *Antigone*, translated by Reginald Gibbons and Charles Segal (New York: Oxford University Press, 2003). See my essay "On the Translation," 37–49. See also my essay "On the Translation" in Euripides, *Bakkhai*, translated by Reginald Gibbons with an Introduction and Notes by Charles Segal (New York: Oxford University Press, 2001), 33–41.

George Steiner, *Antigones* (New York: Oxford University Press, 1984).

Editions consulted include:

All seven of Sophokles' tragedies edited, translated and annotated by Sir Richard C. Jebb (1841-1905), now reprinted and also available online at www.perseus.org.

The Fragments of Sophocles, edited by A. C. Pearson, Cambridge [England], three volumes, 1917. (This was to be the final volume of Jebb's multivolume edition of Sophokles, but he did not live to complete it.)

Sophocles, *Oedipus Rex*, edited by R. D. Dawe, Cambridge [England]: Cambridge University Press, 1982.

Sophocles, *Trachiniae*, edited by P. E. Easterling, Cambridge [England]: Cambridge University Press, 1982.

Sófocles, *Fragmentos*, introduction, translation and notes by José María Lucas de Dios, Madrid: Editorial Gredos, 1983.

Sophocles, edited and translated by Hugh Lloyd-Jones, Cambridge [Mass.]: Harvard University Press (Loeb Classical Library, three volumes), 1994, 1996. (I use this edition as my primary source of the originals.)

Notes to the Translations

Allusions or references in the poems are explained at their first occurrence only. About the paired stanzas of the odes, see Introduction, pp. 19–20.

"Aphrodite of Kypros" [fragment 941], p. 25

§ It is not known from which lost play this fragment survives. There is a gap in the text after line 11 of the Greek.

§ "of Kypros," i.e. from Cyprus (as we call it), which was said to be Aphrodite's birthplace, and was the principal site of her cult.

§ "what's inside the breast": From Homer to Sophokles—several centuries—the Greek sense of thought and emotion, as expressed in poetry at least, remained more or less the same. The Greeks did not locate thought and feeling only in the mind; or rather, they seemed to see mind in much more of the body, not the brain alone (and we now know from neuroscience that this is indeed the case). One Greek verb for thinking, *phronein*, for example, puts it in the *phrenes* (plural). In this ode, the word seems to signify the lungs, which were believed to be where love was felt. We can accept the justness of this if we recall our own physical state when in love—all the lightness or other sensation in the chest. Or the *phrenes* can be the chest and midriff generally—seat of both feeling and thought. The mind or soul or spirit of life is the *thymos* (as in our "thymus gland"; or our "dysthymia," which is in fact an ancient Greek word that meant despair or depression). Thoughts or feelings were also in the heart, *kêr*. The word I translate in this line of the fragment as "thought" is *psykhê*, our "psyche." But unlike the Greeks, we interpret this word to mean "soul," because later, by the time of the Greek of the New Testament, this was the common usage (although *psykhê* could also mean "life" and "mind"). See the early essay on this topic, "The organs of consciousness," in R. B. Onians, *The Origins of European Thought* (Cambridge: Cambridge University Press, 1951), and the great deal that has been written about it since then by scholars, philosophers, political theorists, neuroscientists and others.

"On Eros and Aphrodite" [*Antigone* 781–800] p. 26

§ Translated with Charles Segal

§ The chorus of Theban elders sing this ode after the scene of bitter conflict between Kreon, the king, and his son Haimon (who is betrothed to his cousin Antigone), in which Haimon argues against his father's decision to kill Antigone. The chorus seem to imply that Haimon's defense of Antigone is motivated by his sexual desire for her, yet Haimon brings persuasive arguments to the conflict with his father. In its context, this ode has a tragic tone: nothing can be done to save the royal house if Eros and Aphrodite rule Haimon. But out of its context, it can also be read, we see, as a celebration of Eros and Aphrodite. Even though the Antigone of the play displays no affection for Haimon, nor does she even speak his name, the poem itself, apart from the play, gives striking precedence to the erotic energy of the bride.

§ This short ode begins with the male Eros and ends with the female Aphrodite, as if enacting a victory by the feminine over the masculine. Note by Charles Segal from *Antigone* (see "Suggested reading," above), to the passage "love in the gaze [. . .] wedding joy": "The dense language of this passage permits several different interpretations. It can refer to the Greeks' belief that desire is an active force that emanates from the eyes of the loved one, in this case the new bride, and inspires desire in the beholder. Or it can refer to the lover's desire for the bride's beauty, or to the eyes' desire for the bride. It is possible that aspects of all three meanings are present simultaneously. In any case, these lines emphasize the erotic side of marriage, over which Aphrodite presides."

§ Note by Charles Segal from *Antigone*, on the line "rules equally with the great laws": "Editors have suspected a corruption [of the text] because the claims for Eros seem exaggerated and because there is not a full metrical correspondence with the relevant line in the strophe. A more serious problem is that one would expect Eros to be the destroyer or transgressor of these 'laws.' Yet such grandiose claims are appropriate to the hymnic style, and no satisfactory emendation has been suggested. We keep the manuscript text."

"Eros, Impossible to Thwart" [fragment 684], p. 27. From Sophokles' lost play *Phaidra*. Lines spoken by one of the characters.

"The Mighty Kyprian" [*Trakhiniai* 497–530], pp. 28–29

§ In this ode, a chorus of unmarried (Greek *parthenos*) young women of the city of Trakhis recount the contest that was fought for Deianeira by the hero Herakles and the monstrous river god Akheloüs, who took the shape of a bull. At this contest, Deianeira herself sat to one side watching and awaiting the outcome that would determine whether she would be rescued by Herakles and marry him, or would be raped by the god. The judge of the contest—yet also in a way very much a participant, because she causes the contest by arousing lust in the combatants for the mortal girl—was Aphrodite, "the mighty Kyprian." But that contest was long ago, and now Deianeira is anxiously awaiting the arrival of her husband Herakles, who has been away for fifteen months. His return, however, will bring not joy but tragedy. The play enacts a number of striking ideas about eros, civilization, nature, fidelity, oracles, and heroism. The contest between Herakles, the most famous of ancient Greek heroes, and the god in the shape of a bull is represented in other works as well, and represented differently; on its treatment in poems by Pindar and Bakkhylides, compared with Sophokles' on the basis of different poetic values and different audiences, see Bruno Gentili, *Poetry and Its Public in Ancient Greece*, translated by A. Thomas Cole (Baltimore and London: Johns Hopkins University Press, 1988), pp. 119–21.

§ The "son of Kronos" is Zeus.

§ Jebb writes: "Oeniadae was long a centre of anti-Athenian influence in western Greece" (his note to line 509), so for Sophokles' audience, the river god would be seen as that much more of an enemy of the Greek hero Herakles.

§ The "son of Zeus" is Herakles, whose mother was a mortal, Alkmenë.

§ A powerful pun in the last line of the antistrophe (here represented by "joining") plays off two homophonic verbs that might both be translated literally as "to be (together)" but which signify on the one hand sexual intercourse and on the other to meet in battle, with an additional suppressed, opposite meaning, to meet in peace; the second possibility compresses two opposite meanings in itself—Deianeira and Herakles may meet in peace if he wins the contest to sleep with her; or Deianeira may be raped by the god Akheloüs if the latter wins.

§ In line 529 of the Greek, Sophokles uses the same expression ("gone at once") that he uses at line 134 in an earlier ode in this play (in this volume entitled "On Herakles"; see pp. 97–99) when he writes that sparkling night and troubles and wealth can disappear in an instant, thus saying, with this echo, that the calf has disappeared as quickly as good or bad fortune can disappear, in the unpredictable world ruled by the gods. Such repetitions with a difference—of single words or phrases—occur often in the odes within any one play by Sophokles.

"On Man" [*Antigone* 332–75] pp. 33–35

§ Translated with Charles Segal

§ The poem's structure is a four-part progression: man and the great theaters of nature, sea and earth; man and animals; man, culture and thought; man's moral judgment and reverence for the gods.

§ In *Musical Design in Sophoclean Theater* (Hanover, N.H. and London: Dartmouth College and University Press of New England, 1996), William C. Scott notes that the poetic meter of this ode "allude[s] to the meters" of the first ode in the play (not translated in the present volume), with an effect of "support[ing] the characterization of this chorus as adherents to a fundamental set of beliefs" (40). In other words, this poem presents a view of man that is both revolutionary in its ascription to human beings, rather than to gods, of the success of human inventiveness and intelligence, yet also conservative in its acceptance of traditional wisdom.

§ Note by Charles Segal from *Antigone*: This poem, "one of the most celebrated choral odes of Greek tragedy, is known as the Ode on Man. [. . .] Sophocles here draws on contemporary theories of the origins of civilization associated with Sophists like Protagoras and Presocratic philosophers like Democritus. But he also models the opening of the poem on the central ode of Aiskhylos's *Libation Bearers* (458–457 B.C.), substituting a praise of human intelligence for Aiskhylos's accusations of the deadly lust of women. [. . .] Three words of the opening phrase in the translation, *awe, terror*, and *wonder*, translate the ambiguity of the single Greek word *deinon*, which may refer to both Kreon and Antigone, and more broadly, to the ambiguous capacities of human beings generally, who, as the ode says (and as the play shows), may move *both to evil and to good*. The echo of Aiskhylos can evoke the dangerous and destructive passions of women and so point to Antigone. Yet the praise of mankind's control of nature also points to Kreon, particularly because the ode's language of taming, trapping and hunting resonates with the authoritarian language of Kreon and his will to power and domination. [. . .] The pointed rhetorical juxtaposition of *inventive in everything* and *without invention* in these lines encapsulates the play's tragic ambiguity of human power. It is echoed in the similar syntactical pattern of *high in his city . . . outside any city*."

§ Gaia is "highest" in the sense of being the oldest god. Note by Charles Segal to *Antigone*: "See Hesiod, *Theogony* 117–18, 126–33."

"The Human Lot" [fragments]. pp. 36–41

I. Fragments 591, 849 (Greek *aulos* might mean pipe, flute, or reed instrument), 593, 868, 681 (a common maxim among the Greeks), 434, 502 (perhaps from a messenger's narration), 354, 940, 350, 584, 488 (another Greek maxim), 320

II. Fragments 961, 356 (here Sophokles has versified in his own way an inscription on the temple of Apollo at Delphi), 856 (another Greek maxim), 735, 870, 873

III. Fragments 833, 918, 834, 954 (Sophokles joins together the conflicting maxims 918 and 954 in the speech by Aias translated in this volume; see p. 93)

IV. Fragments 722, 795, 554, 587, 157, 431, 334, 63, 767, 269a (in part; this fragment is in a very elliptical state due to its survival on half-destroyed papyrus), 885

V. Fragment 927a

VI. Fragments 910, 4, 556, 557 (in part), 13, 828f

VII. Fragments 871 (Lucas de Dios: "Zeus has established that human existence is subject to change, a process which, since Homer, is often compared with natural phenomena, and is frequently described as cyclical" [407]), 393 (the word translated here as "soul," psyche, could also be translated in various contexts—and here there is virtually no context at all—as "mind," "self," "personality," "spirit," or simply "life"; see note, above, on "what's inside the breast," in "Aphrodite of Kypros")

"On Song" [fragment 568], from the lost play *Syndeipnoi* ("those who dine together"), p. 42

§ The Muses are the daughters of Mnemosyne ("Memory") and Zeus. The nine daughters represent the range of human thought and creativity, and in fact the very word "muse" (Greek *mousa*) derives ultimately from an Indo-European root that also gives us such words as "mind," "mental," and "museum." Lethe is the Greek mythological river of forgetfulness leading to Hades, the underworld of the dead: forgetting is the enemy of art and thought. Lloyd-Jones notes that "Life is visualized as a narrow channel between the great oceans of the periods before birth and after death" (III, 285).

"What Sophokles Wrote on Women Was Preserved by Men" [fragments] pp. 43–44

I. 235, 339 (from a play containing a dialogue between Jason and Medea; here perhaps Medea is asking Jason for a sworn promise), 679, 64 ("Argive" means someone from ancient Argos, and by extension, of the region called Argolis; in the heroic age of which Homer tells and which Sophocles retells in his own way, some of the Greeks who go to war under Agamemnon against Troy are Argives)

II. 838

III. 307 (The Greek word *polypous* can mean "sea-polyp," "octopus," "cuttlefish"—creatures that change their color depending on their surroundings; the connotations of the utterance might change accordingly; this familiar maxim was also applied by men to men, with regard to political situations; see Gentili's chapter 8, "Poet-Patron-Public: The Norm of the Polyp"; the questions here include whether to read *anêr* as "man" or as "husband," and whether the advice is that a woman should *imitate* the "color" of a man's thoughts, in which case the "rock" is the man, or whether as either prey or predator she should *disguise* her thoughts with protective "coloration."), 306, 932

IV. 189, 682, 942, 811 (this sentiment has several variations in Greek)

V. 583 (from the lost play *Tereus*, about that king of Thrace, his Athenian wife Prokne, and her sister Philomela; these lines are spoken by Prokne, who is now far from Athens); 663

"Fragments of *Thamyras*" [most of the fragments 237–245; the one-word fragments are not in Lloyd-Jones but are added here from Pearson], pp. 45–46

§ I have provided the epigraph from Homer in order to sketch in the myth.

§ In this lost play, the tragic character Thamyras (or Thamyris) would have fallen because of his insolence toward the divine Muses. The play was set near Mt. Athos, but ancient sources disagree on the geography of the travels of Thamyras. Among the unreliable ancient anecdotes about Sophokles, one holds that he himself played the lyre in the production of this play. Pearson: "Athos, like other high places, was honoured as a sanctuary of Zeus" (note on 237).

§ Several instruments are mentioned: Greek lyres had seven strings, but the harps or lyres mentioned here are the *plektis*, with twenty strings, and the *magadis*, also with twenty strings, both from Lydia, in Asia Minor—that is, like other elements in ancient Greek culture, they were imported from the east; also mentioned is the *trígônos*, a triangular harp or lyre.

§ Like all too many fragments of and passages in the plays, the Greek phrase about Autolykos (whose name suggests a "lone wolf") is evidently corrupt; some scholars have conjectured that the wording ought to be emended—as it can be—so that it matches other Greek mentions of Autolykos's father as Hermes, the god "who goes under the earth" in his role as psychopomp of the dead, leading them to Hades. (Since Hermes possessed among others powers that of thievery, he is an appropriate father to Autolykos, who grows up to perpetrate his own notorious thefts.)

§ *kánnabis* is the Greek word for hemp; Pearson: "the allusion to hemp— probably to hempen garments—fits the Thracian atmosphere of the play."

§ The word "rules" is my translation of Greek *nomoi*, which can mean laws, customs, or songs or odes. Greek music was melodic without harmony or polyphony, and was seen as related to the realm of the divine. Gentili: "Airs or musical compositions were called *nomoi* (norms, laws, conventions)" (see 25ff). This last fragment is uncertain. I follow Lloyd-Jones's reading of the Greek, but others read different words meaning not that a desire for the sound of pleasurably maddening music makes the speaker of these lines rush to a public place where there will be song, but that the speaker himself is seized by a desire in his own throat to sing. See Pearson on fragment 245.

"On Sleep" [*Philoktetes* 828–32], p. 47

§ This is an excerpt from the chorus's sung dialogue with Neoptolemos. Sophokles' play dramatizes the embassy of Odysseus and Neoptolemos to the remote island where the king and archer Philoktetes had been abandoned by the Greek warriors on their way to Troy because a snake had bitten his foot, causing a festering, stinking sore that would not heal; Philoktetes has been continually crying out in pain from this wound for ten years. Odysseus and Neoptolemos have come now to bring Philoktetes back to Troy because of the prediction of a seer that with both Neoptolemos, who is the young son of Akhilleus, and Philoktetes and his famed bow, the Greeks will finally win their war. The chorus are the sailors who have come with their leader Neoptolemos and with Odysseus to bring Philoktetes to Troy.

§ I mentioned in the Introduction that ancient Greek poetry makes no use of end-rhyme. However, the texture of Sophoklean poetry, like most poetry in ancient Greek, may be very dense with repetitions of sounds within the lines. In *How to Kill a Dragon: Aspects of Indo-European Poetics* (Oxford and New York: Oxford University Press, 1995), Calvert Watkins points out the extraordinary musical density of this little passage by marking (some of) the transliterated phonetic repetitions (515):

> **OD**unas **AD**aēs hupn**ED′**;
> **A**daēs . . . **A**lgeōn;
> ad**AĒS** . . . eu**ĀĒS**;
> alge**ŌN** . . . euai**ŌN**, euai**ŌN**, **ŌN**aks;
> elth**OIS** . . . antiskh**OIS** . . . m**OI**;
> ōna**KS** . . . anti**SK**hois;
> t**ĀN**d, aigl**ĀN**, h**Ā** . . . ta **NŪN**;
> **T**and′ . . . **T**e**T**a**T**ai **T**anūn;
> **AI**glan . . . tetat**AI** . . . p**AI**ōn.

The whole is finally demarcated, bounded by a phonetic *dúnad* or closure between the first word and the last [. . .], which transforms these lines of the chorus from a sequence into a set:

>   hú**PN**
>   **P**aio**N**

An adept at the genre of the paean, Sophocles here proves his skill in the poetics of another age [i.e., a time much earlier than his own, since this poetic device is thousands of years old; or in the case of Celtic poetry, a time later than his own that still preserved this practice]. The poem contains 49 syllables, of which no less than 38 participate in a phonetic repetition figure [. . .].

"The Odes of *Oidipous Tyrannos*"

As the play unfolds, the five odes in *Oidipous Tyrannos* express the sequence of the intense emotions of the chorus of Theban elders, representing the citizens of Thebes, so these odes can be read as a poetic sequence. They maintain a consistent focus on Oidipous, and are linked to each other not only dramatically and thematically, but also by poetic devices—especially repetitions of certain words and ideas, which I too have repeated in English. The odes in *Antigone*, by contrast, are much more independent of each other, and some stand at a more oblique angle to that tragedy.

(1) "The Chorus Plead for Divine Aid" [*Oidipous Tyrannos* 151–215], pp. 51–53

§ This first ode is the "parados," sung by the chorus as they enter the performance area, the "orchestra." It is a large ode. The first pair of stanzas—strophe a and antistrophe a—are an invocation; the second pair, a description of the crisis caused by a plague, ending with a plea to divine power; the third pair contain more pleas.

§ The city of Thebes is afflicted by a plague. Oidipous, the ruler since he defeated the murderous sphinx that had already plagued (we might say metaphorically) the city, seems to act as if he, a human being, can defeat the plague of illness, too, without need of divine oracles or assistance.

Strophe a and antistrophe a:

§ The Greek name of such a hymn of appeal, *paian* (*paean* in Latin and now English), also evokes an early god's name spelled in the same way—perhaps a precursor of Apollo. A paean was specifically aimed at Apollo, the god of prophecy and music, who in this ode is not named but is identified implicitly (line 1) as the oracular spokesman of Zeus, his father, and by the epithets "Delian Healer" and "Phoibos" (Latin "Phoebus"; see below).

§ Pytho is another name for Delphi, the oracular site and temple on Mt. Parnassos; it is rich because of the many gold offerings that have been dedicated at the oracle. Pytho (our "python") was a snake-monster or dragon (in Greek, the same word is used for both) killed by Apollo, who then made her lair the site of his oracle; thus the place itself was called Pytho. In such a contest there is the familiar mythological linking of the female with the earth and the male with the sky (or a realm close to the sky, namely, the mountain dwelling of the gods, Olympos).

§ Jebb: "The Delphian Apollo is also Delian—having passed, according to the Ionic legend, from his native Delos, through Attica, to Delphi (Aesch. *Eum.* 9)" (note on line 154).

§ Artemis, Apollo's twin sister, was also born on Delos. Named in the antistrophe, she is invoked here again by the cry of *iê!* that was also used in line 4 when the chorus cries out to her brother.

§ The epithet Phoibos ("Phoebus" in Latin) associates Apollo with the sun, hence its meaning, "radiant." Apollo is "far-striking" as an archer.

§ The center point of the earth was understood to be the "navel of the earth," the *omphalos*, a sacred stone in the temple at Delphi, the earthly midpoint.

Strophe b and antistrophe b:

§ The "god of the west" is presumably Hades.

§ Regarding the "altar–shores," see the quotation from Charles Segal, above, "Introduction" p. 15.

§ The Healer is again Apollo, and the "golden daughter of Zeus" is Athena.

Strophe c and antistrophe c:

§ The destructive war god Ares is associated with the killing plague that has come to Thebes. He burns people with radiated light, perhaps an image for the fevers of sickness.

§ The wife of Poseidon, the god of the sea, is Amphitritë, who is referred to by name in the Greek rather than being identified as the wife of Poseidon, as I call her for clarity's sake; her mansion is the Atlantic, far beyond nearby waters. To either the far western waters of the Atlantic, or the remote eastern waters of the Black Sea, the chorus members plead for Ares to be sent by the other gods.

§ The exact meaning and relevance of what I have translated as "If night fails / To accomplish something, / Day comes to it in time" are obscure.

§ In Greek there is wordplay on the epithet "Lykian": in the first line of the antistrophe it is an epithet for Apollo as the god of light, and later in the antistrophe it is the name of the region Lykia (in Latin, Lycia), a coastal region of Asia Minor. Jebb on Apollo: "properly the god of light (*luk*), whose image, like that of Artemis, was sometimes placed before houses, so that the face should catch the first rays of the morning sun" (note on line 203). Jebb also says that Artemis is often represented as holding a torch in each hand (note on line 207).

§ At the end, Ares is evoked without being named; the chorus members are calling on Zeus to punish not a mortal but another god—which is a lot for a mortal to ask.

§ Bakkhos (Dionysos) "shares his name" with Thebes in that he is closely associated with this city of his mother, Semele, and is seen as the city's protector.

§ Bakkhai (maenads) are female worshippers of Bakkhos (Dionysos).

(2) "But What Does the Seer Teiresias Prove against Oidipous?" [*Oidipous Tyrannos* 463–511], pp. 54–56

§ This second ode in the play is the first in which the chorus stand at the center of the performance area, the "orchestra," and sing and dance. It is the first *stasimon*, or "standing ode" (rather than a marching ode like the one the chorus sang when they entered).

§ The first half of this poem articulates the desire to find the murderer who, even if he is elsewhere, as the chorus assume, has morally polluted Thebes. The second half expresses the fear the chorus feel now that Oidipous has been accused by an impeccable moral authority, Teiresias, but also expresses the chorus's great loyalty to Oidipous. The chorus's thoughts about the ambiguous oracle remain troubled.

§ Scott seems to suggest (128–29) that as the meter of the poem in the second strophic pair of stanzas goes from loose to regular, the ode represents rhythmically the tension among members of the chorus between what they fear and what they hope.

§ Strophe a: "the son of Zeus" is Apollo.

§ Same stanza: Here is the first instance (of several) of the word "foot" (Greek *pous*) in the odes, a word that is also the last syllable of Oidipous's name.

§ Same stanza: Dawe notes that the Kêres are "avenging spirits close to, or even identified with, the Erinyes (Furies)" (note on line 472).

§ Antistrophe a: Parnassos is the mountain on which Delphi is located. In the same stanza, the foot of the bull, a figure for Oidipous, is mentioned.

§ Strophe b: The Greek translated here as the "great repute" of Oidipous might instead mean Oidipous's public decree that Kreon and Teiresias have conspired against him. Probably both meanings are available. The "wise interpreter" at the beginning of this stanza is the seer Teiresias. Just before the chorus sing this ode, Teiresias responds to Oidipous's anger at him for speaking the truth, by threateningly but obliquely accusing Oidipous himself of being a threefold criminal—brother to his own children, son of his own wife (or husband of his own mother), and killer of his own father.

§ Same stanza: Polybos is the dead king of Corinth, whom Oidipous mistakenly thinks is his father, so the strife between the son of Polybos and the family of Oidipous's grandfather, Labdakos (i.e., the family of the Labdakids) was in fact the fatal encounter between Oidipous and his own true father, Laios, of whose murder Oidipous will later appear to be proven guilty. The members of the chorus wonder whether to "take the side of the Labdakids," that is, the family of the dead king Laios, against Oidipous; they do not yet know, nor does Oidipous, that he himself is a Labdakid. This family turns on itself in marriage and in murder (later, as predicted in *Oidipous at Kolônos* and as related in *Antigone*, Polyneikes and Eteokles, the sons of Oidipous, will kill one another).

§ Antistrophe b: Sophokles uses two different words for "man": first *brotos*, "mortal," which implicitly distinguishes man from the immortal gods, then *anêr*, "man," which implicitly distinguishes him from either woman or boy; there is a third word, too, in Greek, *anthrôpos*, which implicitly distinguishes man from beasts.

§ Near the end of the ode, the "maiden with wings" is the Sphinx whom Oidipous defeated; it was as reward for this that he was made the ruler of Thebes, and married the queen, a widow.

(3) "On Purity, Insolence, and Punishment" [*Oidipous Tyrannos* 863–910], pp. 57–59

§ This is the second stasimon. Now the elders are very troubled. Oidipous has recounted his killing of an older man, a stranger, in a wagon, together with his attendant, because they had struck at him to make him get out of their way. (This will turn out to have been Laios, the former king, who was on his way to Delphi to consult the oracle again about the earlier prophecy that he would be killed by his own son.) But Oidipous, clinging to the hope that a witness to the killing of Laios will tell a different story, has sent for that witness. The chorus sing in a veiled way of the possibility that Oidipous himself, whom they admire and respect, has in fact been arrogant, impious, reckless and wanton. Yet they plead for the old oracles about Laios, his wife Iokaste, and their child to be proven right. If they are not, then human reverence for the gods will decline (as will be noted, below).

§ Scott writes, "The intensely complex interweaving of religious, political and metaphorical language creates an ode that is difficult to interpret, but leaves no doubt as to the singers' earnestness, the breadth of their ethical view, and the urgency of their doubt. [. . .] Appropriately the meters of this highly organized ode are tightly structured. [. . .] Further, the chorus structures its statement of faith symmetrically in a completed strophic form" (134, 135).

§ Strophe a: This mythological account of the origin of supernal laws is that they were fathered by Olympos (i.e., the high mountain and heavenly realm of the gods) on the aether (here gendered female, meaning the highest skies). "Supernal" is a poor English translation of the Greek word, *hypsipodes*, meaning literally "high-footed" and figuratively "bred on high," thus "lofty," "sublime." "Foot" appears again in antistrophe a: "useless feet." In this same stanza, the wording of the opening sentence, "Insolence begets a tyrant," suggests in Greek the planting of seeds. In Thebes this has an ominous undertone, because it calls to mind the founding of Thebes by Kadmos, who after killing a dragon or great snake guarding a sacred spring was instructed by Athena to pull out the dragon's teeth and plant half of them. From these seeds sprang ferocious warriors who began to kill each other. "Insolence" is one way to translate *hubris*, which is a violation of respect for the gods, an overweening mortal trespass on divine power or prerogative. Perhaps Laios was insolent when, despite the warning of Apollo's oracle, he engendered a son; perhaps Oidipous has become insolent because he is powerful, and his insolence has made him tyrannical (for instance, he summarily condemns Kreon to death, but then is persuaded to back off).

§ Strophe b: What "must not be touched" is clearly Iokaste, if the toucher is Oidipous.

§ Same stanza: The question about the "arrow shafts of his own [i.e., Oidipous's] overwrought mind" represents one choice among several about how to translate some very puzzling and apparently corrupted lines. Dawe says in his commentary: "An impossible line to understand." Perhaps the arrow shafts meant are those that the gods might now be sending at Oidipous. Perhaps they are not from within himself but instead they come into him, piercing his *thymos*—"mind" or "heart" (see note on "what's inside the breast," in "Aphrodite of Kypros," above). But there are good dramatic and psychological reasons to think of Oidipous as the victim of his own arrogance, as the poem says. Like the action of *Antigone*, that of *Oidipous Tyrannos* could plausibly be accounted for without the intervention of gods.

§ Same stanza: When the chorus asks why they should any longer "bother to give the gods glory by dancing," they are referring to the religious practice of dancing as a ritual of worship. Note that they are singing this line *while* dancing—asking in effect if they should not simply stop at this very moment in the midst of the performance of the tragedy. But they continue by singing the next stanza in answer to their own question, dancing as if in order to make the gods true and real within the *drama* of the play set in Thebes and also in the *performance* in the theater of Dionysos in Athens—as if, in both mythical Thebes and fifth-century Athens they must restore godly power over a human realm disordered by irreverence. This is a "metatheatrical" moment in the play.

§ Antistrophe b: The "navel of the earth," the *omphalos* stone at Delphi first mentioned in the first ode, is mentioned again here. Abai is in Phokis, the mountainous central region of Greece that contains Delphi and Parnassos. Olympia is the site in the Peleponnesos where the Olympic games were held, and where there was an important altar to Zeus.

§ Same stanza: The "old prophecies concerning Laios" are the oracles recounted in this tragedy, predicting that Laios would be killed by his son; hence the decision of Laios to deliberately allow the infant Oidipous to die by exposure on mountain heights, a decision thwarted by the kindness of the servant to whom the task was delegated, who instead gave the infant to another man—and thus began the roundabout journey of Oidipous from Thebes to Corinth as an infant and back again as a young man. But if oracles are not obeyed by men (Laios violated his oracle of warning, as noted above, by engendering Oidipous) and are not proven true by outcomes attributable to the gods (as happens in the play—but this choral ode is sung before that outcome is clear), then religion is dying.

(4) "A Dance of Hope" [*Oidipous Tyrannos* 1086–1109], pp. 60–61

§ This is the third stasimon. As one sees in *Antigone*, too, where late in the play the chorus sing an ode of unrealistic and unjustified hope for a good outcome, the elders now hope, against all evidence, that Oidipous, since clearly he is not the biological child of Polybos after all, will be revealed instead as the child of a god (Pan, Apollo, Hermes, or Dionysos). If so, then he is truly the protector of Thebes, not its destroyer. This ode expresses a desire to naturalize the hero Oidipous to Thebes in some other way—not by family but by attributing to him a mythological birth and childhood.

§ Scott says that the meter of this poem alludes to the meter of the first ode, in which the chorus pleaded with the gods to save Thebes from the plague. First they "called on the gods to come as warriors against the plague," and now they ask the gods to show that Oidipous is himself the son of a god "and can bring honor to Cithaeron as his birthplace" (137).

§ Strophe: Olympos is the mountain on which the Greek gods reside. Kithairon is the mountain that dominates the city-state of Thebes below it, and on which Oidipous was to be exposed and die as an infant. The geography of the cities and mountains of the mythological era is not, however, real: Olympos is in northern Greece and Kithairon cannot be seen from Thebes.

§ Antistrophe: This stanza is addressed to Oidipous. The association of Apollo with Loxias, one of his oracular sites, emphasizes his oracles, which were notoriously ambiguous or incomprehensible; the word "Loxias" is related to others suggesting obliqueness both literal and figurative.

§ Same stanza: Charles Segal points out the echo of "high-footed laws" (*nomoi*—third ode [second stasimon]) here in the mountain pastures (*agronomoi*); that is, the celestial laws seem to have fallen to earth, laws of the gods having now become merely the behavior (grazing) of beasts (*Sophocles' Tragic World*, 192). This kind of turning of the meaning of a word—which Sophokles does often—by bringing it back in a different morphological form is one of the oldest (yet still current) devices of poetry.

§ Same stanza: The Lord of Mt. Kyllênê (now called Mt. Ziria, in the Peloponessos) was Hermes. As before, the "god of the Bakkhai," that is, of the maenads, is Dionysos.

(5) "Oidipous the Cursed" [*Oidipous Tyrannos* 1186–1222], pp. 62–64

§ The final stasimon. Soon after singing the previous ode, the elders of the chorus are thrown into despair by the conclusive revelation that Oidipous is indeed the murderer of his father and the husband of his mother. With familiar dejection the chorus sing of the complete turn of fortune of Oidipous—from heroic savior of the city of Thebes to the most monstrous, infamous, and wretched of men.

§ Scott says that the contrast in meter between this ode and the previous one "mirrors the contrast in content. In the third stasimon the elders sang a single organized strophic pair to a dactylic meter referring metrically to the parados, where they eagerly entrusted themselves to their gods." But here "there is a sharp contrast between the two strophic pairs [. . .], one of which is designed as a metrical unit while the other is sharply split into sections. [. . .] Both meter and content become disjointed in the second strophic pair [. . . .] Sophocles uses a weakened musical structure, for the first time in the play, to characterize the chorus' inability to reconcile its earlier views with present events" (140–42).

§ Strophe a: The "generations" are also all tribes and nations.

§ Antistrophe a: The "oracle-chanting maiden with sharp curving claws" is the Sphinx that had been terrifying Thebes and killing those who encountered it; Oidipous, having defeated the Sphinx, was acclaimed as king by the Thebans. Out of respect and admiration, here the members of the chorus call Oidipous their "king" rather than a "tyrant." (The sphinx is called *parthenos*, "unmarried," which is the same word that describes the chorus of young woman in *Trakhiniai* who surround Deianeira—who was herself *parthenos* as she watched Herakles fight for her against the river god. And of course some of the Greek goddesses—especially Athena, whose huge statue stood in the Parthenon, were *parthenoi* as well. The word evidently evoked a complex group of feelings among men in fifth-century Athens. The Theban sphinx may be young or old—there seems to be no indication of her age—but in either case, her power comes partly from her status as *parthenos*; what she did to men who could not answer her riddle was to eat them.)

§ Strophe b: Because, as King of Thebes, Oidipous unwittingly married his own mother, Iokaste, he has issued from the same womb (the "harbor," in this poem; Sophokles and other ancient Greek poets make frequent use of maritime imagery), which he has in turn impregnated with four more children, his two sons (and half-brothers) and his two daughters (and half-sisters). Thus there are two father-and-children sets for whom Iokaste's womb has served as "harbor"—Laios and Oidipous, Oidipous and his children. As harbors do by nature, the Iokaste harbor has remained fixed, so to speak, while the implied boats—fathers and children—have come in and gone out. The disaster of Oidipous's ill-fated life is unique. Then the poem calls the womb a "furrow"—a more graphic image, and one that Sophokles uses also in *Antigone*, albeit with a different word.

§ Antistrophe b: The last sentence might have the meaning I have represented, or it might mean that Oidipous gave the chorus a new life and now is killing them; this might be the sleep of death. But it is not the chorus who are dying; it is, rather, Oidipous and all in his family who are doomed. Thebes, though, will finally be cleansed of the polluting presence of Oidipous. In Greek the last word in the ode is "eyes"; as soon as the chorus finishes singing this ode, a messenger will arrive to describe Iokaste's suicide and the self-blinding of Oidipous.

"On the Long Life of Oidipous" [*Oidipous at Kolônos* 1211–48], pp. 67–68

The chorus of elders of Kolônos sing this song of proverbial Greek sentiment just before a scene in which Oidipous in anger will curse his sons Polyneikes and Eteokles, and then will become aware that he himself is about to die. In the strophe, "He who helps lead everyone. . ." is Hades, god of death. In his note on line 1225, Jebb cites other texts that echo the proverbial quality of the beginning of the antistrophe, "Not to be born. . ." After the strophe and responding antistrophe, this poem has a single last stanza, an epode. The last lines suggest the four points of the compass.

"On Fate and the Last of the Family" [*Antigone* 582–625], pp. 69–71

§ Translated with Charles Segal.

§ Scott writes that the "musical design of the first part of the play underlines the chorus' efforts to expand its original religious interpretation (parados) to include religious guidance (The Ode on Man, 365–70) [see pp. 33–35, above] and finally religious determinism (the Ode to Zeus, esp. 604–25) [i.e., the present ode]." Scott argues that the change in poetic meter from ode to ode in this play "gives a necessary clue to the growing inadequacy of the chorus' analysis of the episodes" of the action. (45–6).

§ After Antigone is apprehended by guards who had been sent outside the city walls of Thebes to watch over the corpse of her brother Polyneikes, and to enforce Kreon's edict against burying the body under penalty of death, she is imprisoned temporarily by Kreon in the royal house for having defied his edict. The Theban elders of the chorus sing of the tormented history of the family of Labdakos (see notes to the odes of *Oidipous Tyrannos*, above). As soon as they end this song, Kreon's son Haimon enters, and the torments of Kreon's family will begin to grow, as if echoing those of the family of Labdakos.

§ Notes by Charles Segal from *Antigone*:

"*afflictions[. . .] yet earlier afflictions of the dead.* The chorus means that the woes of the living Labdakids, i.e. Antigone and Ismene, are being added to those of the already dead members of the family, from Laios through Eteokles and Polyneikes. It is also possible to construe these dense lines to mean that the woes of the dead Labdakids are being added to those of their living kin, but this is rather less likely.

"*rootstock of the House of Oidipous. . . reaped by blood-red dust of the gods under the earth. . . a Fury in the mind.* These are among the most difficult and controversial lines of the play. The image of the bloody dust 'reaping' or 'mowing down' the root of Oidipous's house is bold, too bold for many editors, who emend the word 'dust' (*konis*, the reading of all the manuscripts) to 'knife' (*kopis*). But the manuscript reading is in keeping with the play's emphasis on the powers of the lower world; and the bloody dust evokes the death of the two brothers, the continuing doom of the house in Antigone's sprinkling of dust over Polyneikes' body, and perhaps also the dust storm in which she performs that burial. The emendation *kopis*, moreover, would refer to a 'chopper,' or sacrificial knife, which does not seem particularly appropriate here. Further support for the manuscript reading comes from Aiskhylos's *Seven Against Thebes*, which focuses on the death of the two brothers and is almost certainly in the background here. Aiskhylos's chorus describes how, at the mutual slaughter of the two brothers, 'the earth's dust drinks the red clotted blood' (*Seven*, 734–37). In the next strophe Aiskhylos's chorus goes on to describe Oidipous's patricide and incestuous marriage, in which he 'endured the bloody *root*' (referring to the incest and its consequences). That strophe ends with 'the madness of mind' that 'brought together' Oidipous and Iokaste as bride and bridegroom (*Seven*, 756–57), and Sophokles may also be referring to that passage in Aiskhylos's antistrophe here, *foolishness of speech and a Fury in the mind.* The Furies, or Erinyes, are the avenging deities of the lower world who typically punish the crime of bloodshed within the family. In this function they are also often the instruments that fulfill a family curse. They typically bring madness upon their victims. Thus, Antigone's *Fury in the mind* here seems to refer to her ritual burial of Polyneikes and its aftermath where (as the chorus sees it) reason and good sense give way to the destructive madness and folly that persist in the house of Oidipous as the result of the inherited curse."

"Oidipous on the Passage of Time" [*Oidipous at Kolônos* 607–23], p. 72

This is from a speech by Oidipous, when he is near death, on the outskirts of the small city of Kolônos (only a twenty- or thirty-minute walk from the center of Athens). The legendary hero Theseus, son of Aigeus, the former king of Athens, has come from Athens to protect Oidipous from the force or importuning of either his son Polyneikes or his brother-in-law Kreon. The former wants his support in his war against his brother (the aftermath of that war is the material of *Antigone*); the latter wants to bury Oidipous's body outside the city walls of Thebes, where according to an oracle his tomb, because it is cursed, will ward off invaders. But because Oidipous has become sanctified by his suffering, and his tomb will be a place linked to divine powers, Kolônos welcomes him, and Theseus—having come out from Athens—protects him. (For the Athenians, mythological Thebes, not far away, was the stage onto which their own political and religious crises could be projected in tragedy.)

"On Behalf of Oidipous" [*Oidipous at Kolônos* 1557–78], pp. 73–74

§ After his years of wandering and suffering, blind Oidipous appears to be about to meet, or even to will, his own death, and the chorus of elders of Kolônos pray that his long suffering for his crimes will earn him at last a safe passage to the underworld of the dead.

§ Strophe: The "goddess who cannot be seen" is Persephone. Jebb points out that this epithet may have to do with the literal meaning of Hades' name in Greek, *Aidês*, that is, "not seen" (note to line 1556). *Aidoneus* is a poetic version of the name Hades. Styx is the name of both the river (also called Akheron) over which the dead were ferried to the underworld, and its goddess, who lived in Hades. The "child of Earth" is probably Thanatos, Death (Jebb's note on line 1574).

§ Antistrophe: Jebb also notes that the "goddesses of the earth" cannot be Demeter and Persephone, who would not be associated with the "beast"

Kerberos (Latin, Cerberus), the dog-monster of Hades, but rather must be the Erinyes (Furies).

"In Praise of Kolônos" [*Oidipous at Kolônos* 668–719], pp. 77–79

§ This exuberant ode delights in describing and celebrating the beauties of Kolônos and its ties to the gods.

§ Strophe a: In one of the myths of Dionysos, he is a goat-child reared on Mt. Nusa (or Nysa)—located by different authorities in different places—and so the holy women who once nursed Dionysos are the Nysaian nymphs who cared for him, which is to say, another kind of maenad, whose name in Greek means women in a state of divine madness of worship of Dionysos.

§ Antistrophe a: Jebb notes that "the symbolism of *narkíssos* in Greek mythology is clear. It is the flower of imminent death, being associated, through its narcotic fragrance, with *narkê* [numbness, deadness],—the pale beauty of the flower helping the thought. It is the last flower for which Persephone is stretching forth her hand when Pluto seizes her,—Earth having put forth a wondrous narcissus, with a hundred flowers, on purpose to tempt her" (note on line 683). He cites the *Homeric Hymns* 5.15. He adds, "as the flower which Cora [Persephone] was plucking when seized, it was associated with their cult from the first, and was one of the flowers which would be most fitly woven into those floral wreaths which, on the wall-paintings, sometimes replace Demeter's more usual crown of corn-ears." The ancient Greek crocus might have been our saffron, but in any case it too was a flower gathered by Persephone. The "great goddesses" are Demeter and Persephone. Aphrodite's "golden reins": she sometimes drove a golden chariot pulled by swans, doves, or sparrows.

§ Strophe b: The "Island of Pelops" is the Peloponnesos. The "self-originating plant" is the olive tree, given by Athena to the Attic Greeks; she commanded it to spring from the ground of the Akropolis. (She is associated with the gray of the underside of the olive leaf—one of her epithets is "gray-eyed," as in this poem). "This land" is Attica—the Greek region of which Athens was the capital. Jebb: "The poet does not mean, of course, that he has never heard of the olive as growing in the Peloponnesus or in Asia Minor. [...] He means that nowhere else has he heard of an olive tree springing from the earth at a divine command, or flourishing so greatly and so securely under divine protection."

§ Antistrophe b: This "son of Kronos" is Poseidon, god of the sea and of horses. About the Nereids, sea-nymphs that escort ships, Jebb notes, "Nêreus and his daughters represent the sea's kindly moods: the Nereids who dance and sing around and before the ship are the waves" (note to line 718).

"The Fullness of the World" [fragments], pp. 80–82
 I. 127, 276, 37, 226, 718, 286 (in ancient Greece, this might be an image of prosperity, or on the contrary an image of ruin and scarcity), 549
 II. 439, 370, 407a, 329
 III. 111, 23, 89
 IV. 475, 563 (probably said of a slave), 859 (Plutarch says Sophokles is describing Trojan warriors in this passage)
 V. 398 (a description of sacrifices made to the gods)
 VI. 586
 VII. 869

"The Sea" [fragments], pp. 83–85
 I. 555, 761, 685, 337, 143, 371
 II. 440, 840, 476
 III. 479 (Palamedes was a legendary inventor—of the alphabet, "weights, numbers and measures" [fragment 432], beacons, navigation by the stars, the games mentioned in this fragment, and other things), 636

"To Dionysos" [*Antigone* 1115–52], pp. 86–87
 § Translated with Charles Segal.
 § Scott writes that this ode is "a simply structured, repeated cry for aid sung to randomly patterned meters" (59). That is, the metrical pattern of the original (or rather the lack thereof) suggests panic.
 § Teiresias has said that the gods are angry because the unburied bodies of the dead attackers of Thebes, who had been led by Polyneikes, are a pollution, and because while Kreon has failed to put the dead properly underground, he has wrongly put a living person there—Antigone, condemned to be walled up inside a tomb. Near the end of the play, after Kreon changes his mind or heart and rushes to rescue Antigone and bury Polyneikes, the Theban elders of the chorus yield—against the evidence of all the signs and events so far—to a fervent hope that Dionysos, the god most associated with Thebes, will now rescue the city from pollution and danger. They sing joyfully to Dionysos, who is also called Bakkhos and Iakkhos. But immediately after the singing of this ode, they will learn that the royal households—that of Oidipous and that of Kreon—have been brought to a bloody end.
 § An ode very rich in mythological background and allusion. Note by

Charles Segal from *Antigone*: "This ode of supplication [. . .] summons Dionysos, patron god of Thebes, to come to his birthplace and save his city by warding off the *disease* of pollution about which Teiresias has just warned. The ode [. . .] answers the parados, the first ode [of this play], which ends with Dionysos and nocturnal [religious] ritual [celebrating the end of war]. Now, however, joyous thanksgiving gives way to anxious prayer, civic choruses in the temples within the city change to a figurative chorus of fiery stars in the heavens, and citizens are replaced by the frenzied female worshippers of Dionysos."

§ Notes by Charles Segal to particular phrases and words:

"*God of many names* Greek gods typically have many epithets to denote their different functions or different local cults, and it is important to address the deity by the appropriate name. So here the chorus invokes Dionysos, in hymnic fashion, by referring to several of his places of worship.

"*Glory of the young wife* [The young mortal] Semele, daughter of Kadmos, is the mother of Dionysos by Zeus and gives birth to him prematurely when Hera, Zeus's Olympian wife, tricks her into asking Zeus to show himself to her in his full divine glory. She is killed by his lightning, but Zeus saves the infant. The myth, told at length in Euripides' *Bakkhai*, is the basis of Thebes's special claim on Dionysos.

"*Kadmos* The founder of Thebes, Kadmos is the father of Semele, Dionysos' mother.

"*Italy* The worship of Dionysos was especially popular in the Greek colonies of Sicily and southern Italy (Magna Graecia, or Great Greece, as it came to be called), which was also noted for its wine production.

"*Eleusinian Demeter, shared by all* Dionysos, in the cult form of Iakkhos (the last word of the ode in Greek), was an important place in the rites of Demeter at the panhellenic sanctuary of Eleusis, on the southern outskirts of Athens. The rites are open to all who undertake initiation (hence *shared by all*) and promise to the initiates a blessed life in the hereafter. Demeter is here paired with her daughter, Persephone, and in fact the rites (which were kept secret) gave a prominent place to the myth of the latter's rescue from Hades by her mother. Both the promise of return from Hades and of some kind of personal salvation that mitigates the pain of death stand in ironic contrast to the events of the play [*Antigone*]." That is, as Segal notes elsewhere, Persephone is a "mythical model" for Antigone herself, who also descends to the underworld when she is still alive, but who is not rescued by anyone, either mortal or divine.

"*Bakkhos* This epithet of Dionysos is used especially in connection with his role as wine god and with his ecstatic cult of frenzied processions and dances.

"*Thebes, mother-city of the Bakkhai* Thebes is the birthplace of Dionysos and therefore is a place where the Bakkhai, the female worshippers of the god in his dances and processions, have special prominence.

"*Ismenos* This river flows through Thebes.

"*pine-torches. . . double peak of rock. . . Korykian nymphs. . . Kastalia flows down* Sophokles here refers to an important aspect of the Theban cult of Dionysos. His *Bakkhai*, or female worshippers, honor the god in a nocturnal procession every other year on the heights of Mt. Parnassos, above Delphi, accompanied by torches, ecstatic dancers, and the tearing apart of wild animals. The *double peak* refers to the twin crags prominent above Delphi, known as the Phaidriades, which these processions pass. In these upland plateaus of Parnassos is also the cave sacred to the Korykian Nymphs, who are closely associated with the god and are here imagined as accompanying these nocturnal processions. The spring of Kastalia flows down from these heights to Delphi below. Its water was sacred and was thought to bring poetic inspiration.

"*ivy slopes of Nysaian hills send forth. . .coast rich with grapes* More cultic details of Dionysos: Nysaian hills refer to Nysa, a mountain sacred to Dionysos located variously in Egypt, Italy, Asia Minor, and Thrace. The ivy, because of its deep green, curling vine, is associated with the god's vital energies and vegetative power, and the grape (with its vines) belongs to Dionysos as the god of wine. The Greek verb for *send forth* (*pempei*) connotes an escort or ritual procession (*pompê*), and Dionysos is often depicted on contemporary vases as arriving in such processions, escorted by nymphs and satyrs. The figurative use here makes it seem as if the god leads his own Dionysian landscape in such a procession.

"*immortal followers cry out the Bakkhic chant* Sophokles is using a verb that means to 'utter *euoi*,' the cry of the Bakkhants in their excited worship of Dionysos. Dionysos is himself sometimes referred to as 'the Euian one,' the god worshipped by the shouts of *euoi!*

"*Your mother, she who was struck by lightning* Semele gives birth to Dionysos amid the lightning flashes of Zeus's majesty.

"*Disease. . . the city. . . and all its people, come cleanse us* The chorus calls on Dionysos to bring an end to the pollution caused by the unburied corpse of Polyneikes, which both is a 'disease' and also may be the fearful cause of diseases [. . .]. The pollution, or *miasma*, is feared as a kind of infectious stain or filth that needs 'cleansing.' [. . .] Scattered references to Dionysos as healer occur in the ancient sources; this is the earliest. In the

Greek, our wording *come cleanse us! Stride. . .* is literally 'come with cleansing foot,' which may be a reference to the cathartic effect of ecstatic Dionysiac dance, given the emphasis on ecstatic dancing throughout the ode.

"*slopes of Parnassos. . . moaning narrows* Dionysos would come to Thebes either from the west via Parnassos and Delphi, where he is worshipped, or from the northeast across the narrow channel of the Euripos, which lies between the mainland of Boeotia and the island of Euboea.

"*Lead the dance of the stars. . . the voices sounding in the night* This beautiful and remarkable image projects into the night sky the dances of Dionysos and his worshippers in their nocturnal processions on earth. The Dionysos who watches *over the sacred ways of Thebes* at the end of the previous antistrophe now extends his presence to vast cosmic distances.

"*show us Your Presence. . . Bakkhantic Nymphs. . . frenzied dance* Dionysos often makes his appearance in sudden, unexpected, spectacular ways, and the Greek verb here, *pro-phanêthi*, implies a request for such a Dionysiac 'epiphany.' These female worshipers and attendants of Dionysos accompany the god in his procession and share the madness or 'frenzy' of his ecstatic dances [. . .]. The word translated as 'Bakkhantic Nymphs' is the Greek *Thyiades*, women or nymphs caught up in the ecstatic worship of Dionysos, from a verb meaning to 'rush or leap furiously.' Sophokles offers his own implicit gloss in the following phrase, 'frenzied dance,' where 'frenzied' or 'maddened,' *mainomenai*, evokes the more familiar term, *mainades*, maenads, literally 'maddened women,' although the Thyiades here are probably to be thought of as nymphs rather than mortal women."

"On the Madness of Aias" [*Aias* 596–645], pp. 91–92

§ Aias (Latin, Ajax), one of the Greek heroes of the Trojan War, was from the island of Salamis. He joined the Akhaian (Latin, Achaean) war expedition to Troy with his own ships and warriors. Sophokles' tragedy is set near Troy, under Mt. Ida, far from Aias's homeland. Furious at having lost honor in being defeated in a contest with Odysseus for the arms of the dead Akhilleus (Latin, Achilles), Aias goes mad, or is made insane by Athena (whose favorite is Odysseus), and although Aias sets out to kill his fellow war captains in revenge for his dishonor, he slaughters instead a herd of cattle. Coming again to his senses he feels great shame, and resolves to kill himself. Sophokles' chorus are Aias's soldiers, who have sailed with him from their homeland to the great Greek military camp on the shores near Troy.

§ Antistrophe a: Two gods, in fact, affect his mind or spirit—Athena in making him mad, but also, when he was heroic, Ares in giving him battle courage; the word "battle" in the translation is the metonym "Ares" in the Greek.

§ Strophe b: For the Greeks, the nightingale was feminine, "the songstress," hence often associated with the lamentation of women over deaths; one of ancient Greek women's social roles was to produce funeral lamentation.

§ Antistrophe b: Aias's father, Telamon, was the son of Aiakos, an earlier Greek hero, so Aias too is a "son of Aiakos."

"Aias's Meditation before Suicide" [*Aias* 646–85], pp. 93–94

§ Aias says these lines to his fellow warriors from Salamis.

§ "Gut" is a translation of *phren*. The word, often used in the plural, means both the muscles of the upper abdomen, and the heart and lungs, which to Greeks were the seats of both thinking and feeling (see note on "Aphrodite of Kypros," above). Thus, when a Greek committed suicide by stabbing himself in the breast, he was not only killing his body, but was also fatally attacking his own thinking and feeling.

§ The goddess with "heavy rage" is Athena.

§ Having met Hector in single combat at Troy and fought him to a draw, which led the two warriors to exchange gifts, Aias now has Hector's sword. See *Iliad* 7.300–305: Hector says "'that any of the Achaians or Trojans may say of us: / "These two fought each other in heart-consuming hate, then / joined with each other in close friendship, before they were parted."' / So he spoke, and bringing a sword with nails of silver / gave it to him, together with the sheath and the well-cut sword belt, / and Aias gave a war belt coloured shining with purple." (The Chicago Homer, http://www.library .northwestern.edu/homer/)

§ The "sons of Atreus" are the two war-kings of the Greek armies, Agamemnon and Menelaos.

"On the Afflicted Philoktetes" [*Philoktetes* 169–90], pp. 95–96

§ See the first note on "Sleep," above, pp. 108–9.

§ Antistrophe: The "creatures with woolly pelt or dappled" are sheep and deer.

"On Herakles" [*Trakhiniai* 94–140], pp. 97–99

§ The as yet unmarried young women of the city of Trakhis, who form the chorus, sing of Deianeira's anxious awaiting of the arrival of Herakles, the greatest of Greek heroes. They ask the sun to reveal where he is, and in antistrophe b they admonish her to accept the anguish of having been abandoned by him and of longing for him, and they urge her to hope for help from Zeus.

§ Strophe a: The "son of Alkmenë" is Herakles.

§ The same stanza: The geographical features ("sea channels [. . .] two continents") are confusing and can be interpreted in different ways.

§ Antistrophe a: The word "body" is a translation of *phren;* see note on "Aphrodite of Kypros," above.

§ The same stanza: The phrase "she for whom two rivals fought" refers to the battle between Herakles and the river god Akheloüs, who took the shape of a bull; this combat is described in the ode "The Mighty Kyprian," pp. 28–29, above.

§ Strophe b: The "rough sea" is "Cretan sea" in Greek; Easterling notes that this body of water "was and is notoriously rough" (note on 112–21).

§ Antistrophe b: Herakles is the son of Zeus, hence the final question of the poem.

Index of First Lines